RUSSIA'S STRATEGIC OBJECTIVES IN THE MIDDLE EAST AND NORTH AFRICA

HEARING

BEFORE THE

SUBCOMMITTEE ON
THE MIDDLE EAST AND NORTH AFRICA

OF THE

COMMITTEE ON FOREIGN AFFAIRS
HOUSE OF REPRESENTATIVES

ONE HUNDRED FIFTEENTH CONGRESS

FIRST SESSION

JUNE 15, 2017

Serial No. 115–41

Printed for the use of the Committee on Foreign Affairs

Available via the World Wide Web: http://www.foreignaffairs.house.gov/ or
http://www.gpo.gov/fdsys/

U.S. GOVERNMENT PUBLISHING OFFICE

25–844PDF   WASHINGTON : 2017

For sale by the Superintendent of Documents, U.S. Government Publishing Office
Internet: bookstore.gpo.gov Phone: toll free (866) 512–1800; DC area (202) 512–1800
Fax: (202) 512–2104 Mail: Stop IDCC, Washington, DC 20402–0001

COMMITTEE ON FOREIGN AFFAIRS

EDWARD R. ROYCE, California, *Chairman*

CHRISTOPHER H. SMITH, New Jersey
ILEANA ROS-LEHTINEN, Florida
DANA ROHRABACHER, California
STEVE CHABOT, Ohio
JOE WILSON, South Carolina
MICHAEL T. McCAUL, Texas
TED POE, Texas
DARRELL E. ISSA, California
TOM MARINO, Pennsylvania
JEFF DUNCAN, South Carolina
MO BROOKS, Alabama
PAUL COOK, California
SCOTT PERRY, Pennsylvania
RON DeSANTIS, Florida
MARK MEADOWS, North Carolina
TED S. YOHO, Florida
ADAM KINZINGER, Illinois
LEE M. ZELDIN, New York
DANIEL M. DONOVAN, Jr., New York
F. JAMES SENSENBRENNER, Jr.,
  Wisconsin
ANN WAGNER, Missouri
BRIAN J. MAST, Florida
FRANCIS ROONEY, Florida
BRIAN K. FITZPATRICK, Pennsylvania
THOMAS A. GARRETT, Jr., Virginia

ELIOT L. ENGEL, New York
BRAD SHERMAN, California
GREGORY W. MEEKS, New York
ALBIO SIRES, New Jersey
GERALD E. CONNOLLY, Virginia
THEODORE E. DEUTCH, Florida
KAREN BASS, California
WILLIAM R. KEATING, Massachusetts
DAVID N. CICILLINE, Rhode Island
AMI BERA, California
LOIS FRANKEL, Florida
TULSI GABBARD, Hawaii
JOAQUIN CASTRO, Texas
ROBIN L. KELLY, Illinois
BRENDAN F. BOYLE, Pennsylvania
DINA TITUS, Nevada
NORMA J. TORRES, California
BRADLEY SCOTT SCHNEIDER, Illinois
THOMAS R. SUOZZI, New York
ADRIANO ESPAILLAT, New York
TED LIEU, California

AMY PORTER, *Chief of Staff*   THOMAS SHEEHY, *Staff Director*

JASON STEINBAUM, *Democratic Staff Director*

———

SUBCOMMITTEE ON THE MIDDLE EAST AND NORTH AFRICA

ILEANA ROS-LEHTINEN, Florida, *Chairman*

STEVE CHABOT, Ohio
DARRELL E. ISSA, California
RON DeSANTIS, Florida
MARK MEADOWS, North Carolina
PAUL COOK, California
ADAM KINZINGER, Illinois
LEE M. ZELDIN, New York
DANIEL M. DONOVAN, Jr., New York
ANN WAGNER, Missouri
BRIAN J. MAST, Florida
BRIAN K. FITZPATRICK, Pennsylvania

THEODORE E. DEUTCH, Florida
GERALD E. CONNOLLY, Virginia
DAVID N. CICILLINE, Rhode Island
LOIS FRANKEL, Florida
BRENDAN F. BOYLE, Pennsylvania
TULSI GABBARD, Hawaii
BRADLEY SCOTT SCHNEIDER, Illinois
THOMAS R. SUOZZI, New York
TED LIEU, California

CONTENTS

RUSSIA'S STRATEGIC OBJECTIVES IN THE MIDDLE EAST AND NORTH AFRICA

THURSDAY, JUNE 15, 2017

House of Representatives,
Subcommittee on the Middle East and North Africa,
Committee on Foreign Affairs,
Washington, DC.

The subcommittee met, pursuant to notice, at 2:10 p.m., in room 2172, Rayburn House Office Building, Hon. Ileana Ros-Lehtinen (chairman of the subcommittee) presiding.

Ms. Ros-Lehtinen. The subcommittee will come to order.

After recognizing myself and Ranking Member Deutch for 5 minutes each for our opening statements, I will then recognize other members seeking recognition for 1 minute. We will then hear from our esteemed panel, and the witnesses' prepared statements will be made a part of the record. Members may have 5 days to insert statements and questions for the record, subject to the length limitation in the rules.

The chair now recognizes herself for 5 minutes.

For far too long, the United States has acted timidly in the face of increased Russian aggression, unwilling to confront Putin for fear of provoking a confrontation, even though Putin, like other tyrants, only responds to a position of strength. And it isn't just the executive branch: Congress has played its role too.

For years, administrations have been offering concessions to Russia, and Congress has allowed this to happen. The Bush administration presented a civilian nuclear cooperation agreement, a 123 agreement to Congress, despite concerns Russia was then providing Iran with nuclear technology and providing Syria with advanced conventional weapons in violation of the Iran, North Korea, and Syria Nonproliferation Act. In fact, the Bush administration had sanctioned state-owned Russian entities for Iran-related violations. I led the effort then to block that agreement. President Bush withdrew the proposed nuclear accord, but only after Russia invaded Georgia.

That didn't stop the Obama administration from falling into the same trap, officially submitting to the U.S.-Russia Nuclear Cooperation Agreement to Congress in 2010, despite overwhelming evidence of Russian involvement in Iran's nuclear and conventional weapons program and congressional efforts to strengthen sanctions against Iran.

Russia repeatedly acted as interference for Iran at the U.N., protecting it from scrutiny and increased sanctions, all the while itself violating U.S. sanctions against the world's foremost state sponsor of terrorism. Yet we fail to hold Russia accountable. In fact, as part of the Obama administration's reset, the U.S. lifted several sanctions against Russia, including sanctions against the arms exporter Rosoboronexport, which admitted it was shipping advanced missile defense systems to Syria.

In 2010, the administration agreed to sign over the control of Uranium One, the U.S. uranium processing facility to the Russian Government. Again, despite overwhelming national security concerns. As then ranking member of this committee, I spearheaded a letter alongside the ranking members of the House Financial Services, Armed Services, and Homeland Security Committees urging the Treasury Secretary to oppose this move.

Another consequence of ignoring Russia's behavior was the decision to overturn the Jackson-Vanik amendment, paving the way for Russia to join the WTO, World Trade Organization, and granting Putin permanent normal trade relations. This was part of the deal with the Devil in order to get the Magnitsky Act signed into law. And though we managed to get that signed into law, an important bill, the previous administration failed to use its authorities to sanction Russia's worst human rights violators.

So where are we now? We have established a long history of failing to use the tools the United States has available to it in order to hold Putin and the Russian regime accountable.

Putin's support for Assad has guaranteed that the conflict will continue and that tens of thousands more will die. His alliance with Iran has given Tehran the tools it needs to one day become a nuclear power with strong conventional arms, including advanced missile defense capabilities. He is bolstering General Haftar in Libya, making it almost certain that no progress toward reconciliation will be made there in the near future. Reports indicate that Russia may be deploying troops or possibly wanting to set up a base at the border of Libya and Egypt. Putin is ensuring that Russia ties itself to the energy and military sectors of many countries in the region, giving him leverage and influence in countries that have viewed us with mistrust since the Arab Spring and the Iran nuclear deal.

Russia is not our ally, not in Syria, not in Iran, not on human rights issues. We should not be afraid to push Putin back. He is a strong man, and tyrants like him only respond to strength, not just perceived strength but actual strength. Russia is fragile, and this show of force is just that, a show by Putin. It is time for the U.S. to reclaim our leadership role on the global stage and, particularly, in the Middle East and with respect to Russia.

Yesterday, the Senate passed an amendment to the Iran sanctions bill that included Russia sanctions. And while I support efforts to hold Russia accountable for its cyber activities and its activities related to Crimea, I hope that this will be only the first step toward a more holistic approach to holding Russia accountable for its activities, which threaten U.S. national security interests and global peace and security.

And with that, I am proud to yield to my ranking member, Mr. Deutch of Florida.

Mr. DEUTCH. Thank you, Madam Chairman. Thank you for agreeing to hold today's hearing.

Russia has been in the news a great deal lately. But what has been absent in much of the reporting is a clear analysis of what exactly Russia's foreign policy objectives are under Putin's rule.

Today, we have a chance to focus on the Middle East where Russia has demonstrated again and again a disregard for human rights and for human life. Russia's posture in the Middle East would be troubling in any context, but given the bizarre relationship between this administration and Russia, it is even more pertinent that we as the United States Congress understand why ceding our role as the leader in the Middle East to Russia runs counter to our own national security interests. And we cannot have a full understanding of this administration's foreign policy until we know more about this administration's ties to Russia.

Russia's relationship with Iran, its support for the Assad regime in Syria, and its willingness to align itself with authoritarians shows brazen disregard for international norms and the rule of law.

Are these decisions made solely to counter American objectives and form a bulwark against the United States? I mean, the Soviet Union was the first country to recognize the Islamic Republic of Iran in 1979, and the relationship between Iran and Russia has remained close ever since. No nation has contributed more to Iran's nuclear programs, sold more weapons to Iran, or been more willing to defend Iran's indefensible actions in international fora. As Iran has worked to destabilize nearly every country in the Middle East, Russia seems willing to overlook every Iranian transgression in pursuit of its own ambitions.

In no Middle East country has Russia done more to deserve international condemnation than in Syria. Not only has Russia propped up Syria's war criminal President with arms and funds, but Putin's forces have actively attacked opposition forces aligned with the United States, as well as countless civilian targets on behalf of the Assad regime. Reports from Aleppo indicate that Russia used bunker-busting munitions to attack hospitals on a regular basis, reducing to rubble underground-held facilities that had been out of reach to Syrian forces.

When Assad ordered chemical attacks on civilian populations in April of this year, the planes flew out of a base shared with the Russians, and one would be hard-pressed not to conclude that the Russians were aware that gas was stored at that base. Yet Russia chose not to condemn the attack, which violated the very agreement Russia helped negotiate to rid the country of chemical weapons, or to apologize for their complicity. Instead, they spent days blocking meaningful U.N. Security Council resolutions condemning this heinous attack on children and babies.

Russian actions in Syria have lent support to Hezbollah, a terrorist organization, and other Iranian-backed militias. There are reports that Russia has provided Hezbollah with long-range tactical missiles, laser-guided rockets, and antitank weapons, and on more than one occasion, Russia has provided air cover for Iran-backed operations.

Oddly, the Russian Ambassador to Israel this week went to great lengths to explain why Russia doesn't consider Hezbollah or Hamas terrorist organizations, stating that they have yet to attack Russia or Russian interests. Claiming his involvement in Syria is a way to prevent the spread of ISIS terrorism, Putin has been willing to cast aside international norms and order to ensure his own political future.

Our President has repeatedly talked about how nice it would be if we could fight ISIS together with Russia, except there is one problem. Russia has repeatedly attacked the very forces the United States has aligned itself with in the fight against ISIS, while supporting the action's very regime that we consider the largest state sponsor of terrorism.

I am not sure we need clearer proof that Russia's strategic objectives in the region are in clear contravention with our own. Is the Kremlin's willingness to align itself with the region's worst actors a projection of strength or, rather, a reflection of Putin's deep insecurities? We have an administration that seems to be willing to give Putin the benefit of the doubt and even to drive policy in the region without much questioning.

We must push back against every effort from this President and his allies to legitimize Russian behavior, or to draw false equivalence between Russian actions and those of the United States, as the President did on national television when asked on Fox News about Putin being a killer.

Even as Russia supported brutal dictators and worked to undermine American alliances, President Trump has complimented Putin, calling him a very strong leader, and benefiting from the Russian interference in our elections, suggested partnership with the Kremlin, shared the closely held secrets of allied intelligence agencies with Russia's top diplomats.

There is obviously a lot more to discuss. Russian activity now spans throughout the region, but I am confident that our conversation today will only solidify the fact that the United States should not, by any means, let Russia drive policy in the critical region in the Middle East.

And I yield back.

Ms. Ros-Lehtinen. Thank you very much, Mr. Deutch.

And I will yield to our members for their opening statements. And if I may start with Mr. Chabot of Ohio.

Mr. Chabot. Thank you, Madam Chair.

The previous administration's withdrawal from America's traditional leadership role left a power vacuum around the globe, one that Putin gladly took advantage of. And unfortunately, we are now paying the consequences.

Putin's engagement in Syria and the Middle East has complicated our own strategy for dealing with ISIS and Iran and a litany of other major issues in the region. As the U.S. works to defeat ruthless terrorist groups, Mr. Putin undermines our efforts the entire way by lending support to the Assad regime, continuing to test the limits of our allies, and supplying weapon systems to Iran.

It is clear that Putin hopes to restore Russia's economic, military, and geopolitical influence around the world by capitalizing on the instability in the Middle East. Putin saw an opportunity to win over regional leaders by questioning the credibility of long-term support from the United States, and to some extent, this strategy has worked. However, I also believe that there are plenty of tools for this new administration to use to bring both stability and balance back to the region, and I hope we discuss some of those today.

And I yield back the balance of my time.

Ms. ROS-LEHTINEN. Thank you so much, Mr. Chabot.

Mr. Connolly of Virginia.

Mr. CONNOLLY. Thank you, Madam Chairman.

And you and Mr. Chabot and my friends, but to listen to both of you, you would never know Donald Trump is in the White House. Apparently, everything going on in the Middle East is the fault of somebody else whose name is not Donald Trump.

You would never know that Donald Trump is under investigation and his campaign is under investigation because of his ties and their ties to Russia. You would never know Russia hacked into our election campaign, verified by all of our intelligence community. You would never know that Donald Trump boasted of firing the FBI director because of the Russia thing with the Russian foreign minister. You would never know that it was Donald Trump that praised Vladimir Putin as a strong man and liked the fact that Putin had said nice things about him.

Could that be enabling behavior? I think so. And I think that is the 800-pound gorilla in the room we need to be talking about. So you can pretend all you want that it is all Obama's fault, but we have got a real-life problem right now in real time in this White House, and that is the Donald Trump Presidency.

Ms. ROS-LEHTINEN. Thank you, Mr. Connolly. An enabler.

Mr. Rohrabacher is recognized.

Mr. ROHRABACHER. Four days ago, it was the 30th anniversary of President Reagan going to Berlin and saying tear down the wall. While having been a senior speech writer for President Reagan for 7½ years, I had a chance to have some input, but I did not write that speech. However, I was the one who smuggled that speech to President Reagan so that the senior staff wouldn't take it out before he had a chance to see it. And once he did see it, he withstood enormous pressure to go there and speak the truth.

Ronald Reagan then led this country to peace with the Soviet Union. Ronald Reagan believed in peace through strength. But let's make it very clear, he believed in peace, and he was the one who brought whatever good chance we have to have peace in that part of the world. He is the one who made it happen.

And I will tell you that what we have right now, and I am afraid I disagree with all of my colleagues, what we hear now is war talk, something that will only lead to war, and it is not leading to treating Russia as a power that we need to negotiate with, as Reagan did, for the cause of peace.

I will tell you right now that I called up Condoleezza Rice early on when I heard that their economy was in such a free fall because the West isolated Russia economically after communism fell. They needed to put their scientists to work. They made an agreement with Iran. And I said, this is horrible. But they have got to do it, because they have to make the money. And I said to Condi, I said, look, let's offer them a deal. They could make two nuclear power plants in Australia or New Zealand, financed by the World Bank, it won't cost a penny, and then they won't have this horrible country, Iran, the mullah regime, with nuclear weapons 20 years from now. You know what she said? She said, that is never going to happen, Dana.

Well, I will tell you this much, we have people who can't get over the Cold War, and they are pushing us toward policies of antagonism and repeated unrelenting hostility that will lead us to war. Ronald Reagan wanted peace in this world, and so do I. This is not the way to a more peaceful world or even a freer world.

Ms. ROS-LEHTINEN. Thank you, Mr. Rohrabacher.

Mr. Lieu of California.

Mr. LIEU. Thank you, Madam Chair and ranking member, for this important hearing on Russian aggression.

I find it highly disturbing that just yesterday, The Wall Street Journal reported our President still questions the intelligence community's assessment that Russia engaged in massive cyber attacks on the United States last year.

I am one of four computer science majors in Congress. I read the classified report. I have had classified briefings, and the President of the United States is simply lying when he says another country could have done it. It was Russia. And we cannot properly respond to Russia if our own President will not accept basic facts. But thank goodness we have Congress. Thank goodness the U.S. Senate today overwhelmingly passed increased sanctions on Russia. I urge the House of Representatives to do the same.

We had a foreign power commit hostile acts against this country. That is not acceptable.

I yield back.

Ms. ROS-LEHTINEN. Thank you, Mr. Lieu.

Mr. Kinzinger.

Mr. KINZINGER. Thank you, Madam Chair.

I guess we are going to be in a debate over the administration and not Russia. I will remind everybody, though, that President Trump, actually, is the person that enforced the red line in Syria and destroyed an airfield as a result of these chemical weapons.

Madam Chair, thank you for doing this.

And I thank our guests for being here and giving us your time.

I just want to say, in my opening statement, that Russia has blood on their hands in Syria as well as many other places.

In 2015, America mistakenly and tragically bombed a hospital in Afghanistan. And as a result, the world rightfully called that out, and America made amends; we found ourselves accountable. But every day, medical facilities, hospitals, places where innocent people live and work and simply try to exist in their life are bombed by the Assad regime and backed and bombed by the Russian regime. This is pure and despicable evil.

When our country makes a mistake, we hold ourselves accountable to it and try to make sure we do it better next time. When Russia—they don't make mistakes. They target with precision-guided munitions innocent lives. This is not a country that we can put an olive branch out to and say, you are just like us. You are also a great power. This is a country with an economy the size of Italy.

With that, Madam Chair, I will yield back.

Ms. ROS-LEHTINEN. Very eloquent. Thank you, sir.

Mr. Cicilline of Rhode Island.

Mr. CICILLINE. Thank you, Chairman Ros-Lehtinen and Ranking Member Deutch, for calling this important hearing today.

And thank you to our distinguished witnesses for offering your testimony.

I want to especially thank you, Mr. Kara-Murza, and say how glad I am to see you here healthy and as outspoken as ever, drawing light to the Russian Government's activities at home and around the world. Your bravery in the face of intimidation is an example to us all and a reminder of how lucky we are as Americans to be able to speak our mind, question our Government, and call out corruption when we see it. We thank you for your continuing willingness to speak out.

There is no doubt that Russia is seeking to expand its influence and reach throughout the Middle East. While I hope that we can partner with Russia and the horrific conflict in Syria, we have to remember that their goals in the region are not the same as ours.

We seem to have an administration that wants to give Russia the benefit of the doubt, despite years of evidence that they will use this to manipulate events to their benefit. Moreover, the overwhelming budget cuts proposed by President Trump will leave our foreign policy apparatus decimated and unable to respond, namely, to crises and provocations. By ceding our leadership role around the world so thoroughly, we will be giving Vladimir Putin the opening he has so desperately sought to create over the last dozen years to increase his power and influence in the Middle East.

I hope our witnesses can shed some light on Russia's intentions in the region and suggest steps that Congress can take that will ensure that American interests and national security are protected.

And I will end with one expression of concern, and that is that the Senate passed some strong sanctions yesterday. And it is already being reported that the White House is reaching out in an effort to weaken these sanctions. And I hope that we can send a very strong message that the Congress of the United States is very united in ensuring that severe sanctions are put into place and the Russians are held fully to account.

And with that, Madam Chairman, I yield back.

Ms. ROS-LEHTINEN. Thank you. Well put. Thank you, Mr. Cicilline.

Mr. Schneider.

Mr. SCHNEIDER. Thank you, Madam Chairman and ranking member, for calling this hearing, Russia's Strategic Objectives in the Middle East and North Africa.

The Middle East and North Africa is a region that our interests run both deep and broad, as is going to be said, having read the advanced testimony, history matters. I don't want to take away something you said, but history does matter here, and it is important to understand the history of the region, the history of different interests in this region. I look forward to hearing from the witnesses. Again, thank you for being here.

But I think we also have to look at this in the context of a discussion that is taking place in this chamber, that is taking place broadly in the country, and that is the President's desire to cut our investment in diplomacy and in development. It is a three-legged stool, and if we are going to promote our interests in this region, we need to continue to invest in diplomacy and development as well as defense. And I hope the witnesses will be able to touch a bit on that.

I know we are also going to talk about the sale of weapons into the region and how that plays out, and I think that is an important issue that we understand.

And finally, I just want to associate myself with my colleague from Rhode Island's remarks about the concern on sanctions. It is important that we continue to push back on Russia's interests and Russia's efforts to destabilize this region. Again, not to take anything away from what the witnesses are going to say, but the sense that this is a zero-sum game, if Russia seeks to win, we have to lose, we can't let that be the case. We have to work with our allies to secure our interests.

And with that, I yield back.

Ms. ROS-LEHTINEN. Thank you, Mr. Schneider.

Any other members wish to make a statement?

And now I am pleased to introduce our wonderful set of panelists. I am delighted to welcome my friend and a true hero of democracy, as Mr. Cicilline referred to him, Mr. Vladimir Kara-Murza, who currently serves as the vice chair of Open Russia, a Russian pro-democracy movement. He was a long-time colleague and adviser to opposition leader Boris Nemtsov. And here he is. And this is an actual poster that was used with the bullet holes there. Thank you.

He currently chairs the foundation that bears Nemtsov's name. In response to his activism and opposition, Vlad was poisoned, not once but twice, by the vile Putin regime.

Putin's cronies continue cracking down on dissidents. Just a few weeks ago, his regime detained a popular opposition leader for simply walking down the street and protesting with his presence. Many people involved are likely eligible to be added to the Magnitsky list. We must show Putin and his henchmen that they will not get away with these abuses.

So thank you, my friend, for continuing to stand up against oppression. We all look forward to your testimony, Vladimir.

And next, we would like to welcome Ms. Anna Borshchevskaya— I am so proud, I am going to say it again, Borshchevskaya—who serves as the Ira Weiner Fellow at The Washington Institute, focusing on Russia's policy toward the Middle East. She is also a fellow at the European Foundation for Democracy and was previously with the Peterson Institute for International Economics and the Atlantic Council.

We look forward to your testimony. Thank you.

And finally, we want to re-welcome Mr. Brian Katulis. Saying that right, too. Mr. Katulis is a senior fellow at the Center for American Progress, where his work focuses on U.S. national security strategy and counterterrorism policy. His past experience includes work at the National Security Council and the U.S. Departments of State and Defense during President Bill Clinton's administration.

Welcome back. We look forward to your testimony.

And, Mr. Vladimir Kara-Murza, we will begin with you, Vlad. Welcome.

STATEMENT OF MR. VLADIMIR KARA-MURZA, VICE CHAIRMAN, OPEN RUSSIA

Mr. KARA-MURZA. Madam Chairman, thank you very much for your kind introduction. Far too kind, as always. Thank you also for your leadership here on this Hill for so many years on issues that are so important for so many people. And thank you, in particular, for your leadership.

You mentioned Boris Nemtsov in your opening remarks, and thank you for your leadership in sponsoring the House bill, H.R. 1863, that would designate the space in front of the Russian Embassy here in Washington, DC, as Boris Nemtsov Plaza to commemorate him and his memory. This is very important to very many people.

Thank you, also, to the member of the subcommittee, Mr. Connolly, for cosponsoring this same piece of legislation.

Chairman Ros-Lehtinen, Ranking Member Deutch, esteemed members of the subcommittee, thank you so much for holding this important and timely hearing and for the opportunity to testify before you.

Our subject today is Russia's strategic objectives in the Middle East. And I think before we discuss the substance, it is important also to clarify the terms. What we are talking about today are the objectives of Vladimir Putin's government. For many Russians, including myself, it is a very uncomfortable equivalence to make between our country and the current regime in the Kremlin that has not resulted from democratic elections.

The Kremlin's involvement in the Middle Eastern affairs today is the most active it has been since the heyday of the Cold War.

Just like Hafez al-Assad, with whom Soviet leader Leonid Brezhnev professed to be "fighting shoulder to shoulder," was Moscow's ally in the 1970s and 1980s, so was his son, Bashar al-Assad today. From the start of the internal conflict in Syria in 2011, Mr. Putin has been a staunch defender of the Assad regime, providing it not only with political support and diplomatic cover but also, since 2015, with direct military help as the Russian aerospace forces have conducted bombing raids against Assad's opponents.

The Kremlin has blocked eight Syria-related resolutions at the U.N. Security Council. Most recently, on April 13 of this year, Russia's acting U.N. Ambassador, Vladimir Safronkov—and I should add, behaving in a manner more appropriate for a bar brawl than for the U.N. Security Council—vetoed a draft resolution calling for an international investigation into the chemical gas attack in Khan Sheikhoun.

Vladimir Putin's support for the Syrian dictator is consistent with his longstanding hostility to popular movements, not only in the Middle East, but also in post-Soviet countries, like Georgia and Ukraine, where mass protests have toppled authoritarian governments.

In the fates of these strong men driven from power, he sees his own possible fate. In fact, he has himself publicly compared the mass demonstrations that swept across Russia earlier this year when tens of thousands of people went out to the streets to protest against authoritarianism and corruption; most recently just 3 days ago, both to the Arab Spring and to the Maidan revolution in Ukraine. These protests in Russia were met with a very harsh response, with peaceful demonstrators beaten up by riot police and with more than 1,500 people arrested on a single day.

The official foreign policy concept of the Russian Federation that was signed by Mr. Putin mentions "the growing threat of international terrorism." Yet the Kremlin's approach to this issue has been ambivalent at best. For example, unlike the United States and the European Union, the Russian Government refuses to recognize Hamas and Hezbollah as terrorist organizations. This is what Ranking Member Deutch referred to in his opening remarks.

Russian Foreign Minister Sergei Lavrov has met on several occasions with Hamas leader Khaled Mashal. In January of this year, Mr. Lavrov hosted a meeting in Moscow at the foreign ministry for representatives of several Palestinian groups, which included Hamas, Palestinian Islamic Jihad, and the popular front for the liberation of the Palestine that are also designated by the U.S. and the EU as terrorist organizations.

Asked in a recent interview why the Russian Government considers some terrorists to be bad and others good, the Russian Ambassador to Israel, Alexander Shein, responded that, and I quote, "We do not consider them"—meaning Hamas and Hezbollah—"terrorists at all." This comes despite the fact that Russian citizens in Israel have been among the victims of these groups.

With so many cultural, historical, emotional, and family ties between Russian and Israeli societies, and with fully one-fifth of Israelis, including members of Israel's Government, speaking Russian as their first language, it would seem natural that Russia should treat the state of Israel as a close partner. Instead, the Kremlin's principal ally in the region, alongside Bashar al-Assad, is the Islamic Republic of Iran, where Moscow remains the largest supplier of weapons, where it is actively pursuing new contracts in atomic energy, and which it continues to provide for significant diplomatic support.

Vladimir Putin's objectives in the Middle East have been consistent both with his domestic behavior and with his approach to other parts of the world: Support fellow dictators and undermine efforts of democratization, what his foreign policy concept refers to as "ideological values imposed from outside."

Military involvement in Syria has also been used by the Kremlin for the purposes of domestic propaganda, both to divert attention from economic difficulties at home and to back up the claim that Mr. Putin has restored Russia's status as a great power, a claim that is hardly consistent with reality. A reminder of this came just last month as the leaders of what is now known as the G-7 held their annual summit in Sicily, for the fourth time now without Russia, which was suspended from the group of major world powers because of Mr. Putin's violations of international law.

Thank you very much, once again, for the opportunity to testify. I look forward to any questions you may have.

[The prepared statement of Mr. Kara-Murza follows:]

Russia's Strategic Objectives in the Middle East and North Africa
Committee on Foreign Affairs, U.S. House of Representatives
Subcommittee on the Middle East and North Africa
June 15, 2017

<u>Opening Statement by Vladimir V. Kara-Murza</u>
Vice Chairman, Open Russia

Chairman Ros-Lehtinen, Ranking Member Deutsch, esteemed Members of the Subcommittee, thank you for holding this important and timely hearing and for the opportunity to testify before you.

Our subject today is "Russia's strategic objectives in the Middle East," and before we discuss the substance it is important to clarify the terms: what we are talking about are the objectives of Vladimir Putin's government. For many Russians, including myself, it is an uncomfortable equivalence to make between our country and the current regime in the Kremlin that has not resulted from democratic elections.

The Kremlin's involvement in Middle Eastern affairs today is the most active it has been since the heyday of the Cold War. And, just like Hafez al-Assad—with whom Soviet leader Leonid Brezhnev professed to be "fighting shoulder to shoulder"—was Moscow's ally in the 1970s and 1980s, so is his son Bashar al-Assad today[1]. From the start of the internal conflict in Syria in 2011, Mr. Putin has been a staunch defender of the Assad regime, providing it not only with political support and diplomatic cover, but also, since 2015, with direct military help, as the Russian Aerospace Forces have conducted bombing raids against Assad's opponents. The Kremlin has blocked eight Syria-related resolutions at the United Nations Security Council. Most recently, on April 13 of this year, Russia's acting UN ambassador, Vladimir Safronkov—behaving in a manner more appropriate for a bar brawl than the UN Security Council—vetoed a draft resolution calling for an international investigation into the chemical gas attack in Khan Sheikhoun.

Vladimir Putin's support for the Syrian dictator is consistent with his longstanding hostility to popular movements—not only in the Middle East, but also in post-Soviet countries like Georgia and Ukraine, where mass protests have toppled authoritarian governments. In the fates of these strongmen driven from power he sees his own possible fate. Indeed, he has publicly compared the demonstrations that swept across Russia earlier this year—when tens of thousands of people went to the streets to protest against authoritarianism and corruption, most recently just this week—to the "Arab Spring" and to Ukraine's Maidan revolution[2]. The protests in Russia were met with a harsh response, with peaceful demonstrators beaten up by riot police, and with hundreds arrested.

---

[1] *Reuters*, October 5, 1978
http://www.itnsource.com/shotlist//RTV/1978/10/05/BGY511020085/?v=1
[2] *RBC*, March 30, 2017 *(in Russian)*
http://www.rbc.ru/politics/30/03/2017/58dcfb469a794724c89684df

The Foreign Policy Concept of the Russian Federation signed by Mr. Putin mentions "the growing threat of international terrorism."[3] Yet the Kremlin's approach to this issue has been ambivalent. For example, unlike the United States and the European Union, the Russian government refuses to recognize Hamas and Hezbollah as terrorist organizations. Foreign Minister Sergei Lavrov has met with Hamas leader Khaled Mashal on several occasions. In January, Mr. Lavrov hosted a meeting in Moscow for representatives of several Palestinian groups, which included Hamas, Palestinian Islamic Jihad, and the Popular Front for the Liberation of Palestine, also designated by the U.S. and the EU as terrorist organizations[4]. Asked in a recent interview why the Russian government considers some terrorists to be "bad" and others "good," Russian Ambassador to Israel Alexander Shein responded that "we do not consider them [Hamas and Hezbollah] terrorists at all."[5] This comes despite the fact that Russian citizens in Israel have been among the victims of these groups.

With many historical, cultural, and family ties between Russian and Israeli societies, and with fully one-fifth of Israelis—including many members of Israel's government— speaking Russian as their first language, it would seem natural that Russia should treat the State of Israel as a close partner. Instead, the Kremlin's principal ally in the region, alongside Bashar al-Assad, is the Islamic Republic of Iran, where Moscow remains the largest supplier of weapons; where it is actively pursuing new contracts in atomic energy; and which it continues to provide with significant diplomatic support.

Vladimir Putin's objectives in the Middle East have been consistent both with his domestic behavior and with his approach to other parts of the world: support fellow dictators and undermine efforts at democratization—what his Foreign Policy Concept refers to as "ideological values... imposed from outside."[6] Military involvement in Syria has also been used by the Kremlin for domestic propaganda, to divert public attention from economic difficulties at home and to back up the claim that Mr. Putin has restored Russia's status as a "great power"—a claim that is hardly consistent with reality. A reminder of this came just last month, as the leaders of what is now known as the G7 held their annual summit in Sicily—for the fourth time now without Russia, which was suspended from the group of major world powers because of Mr. Putin's violations of international law.

---

[3] Foreign Policy Concept of the Russian Federation
http://www.mid.ru/en/foreign_policy/official_documents/-
/asset_publisher/CptlCkB6BZ29/content/id/2542248

[4] Ministry of Foreign Affairs of the Russian Federation *(in Russian)*
http://www.mid.ru/ru/foreign_policy/news/-
/asset_publisher/cKNonkJE02Bw/content/id/2597654

[5] *War and Peace*, Channel 9 Israel, June 9, 2017 *(in Russian)*
http://9tv.co.il/video/2017/06/09/67579.html

[6] Foreign Policy Concept of the Russian Federation
http://www.mid.ru/en/foreign_policy/official_documents/-
/asset_publisher/CptlCkB6BZ29/content/id/2542248

Ms. Ros-Lehtinen. Thank you very much. We appreciate it. Good to see you healthy.

And now we will begin with you. Thank you.

STATEMENT OF MS. ANNA BORSHCHEVSKAYA, IRA WEINER FELLOW, THE WASHINGTON INSTITUTE FOR NEAR EAST POLICY

Ms. Borshchevskaya. Chairwoman Ros-Lehtinen, Ranking Member Deutch, honorable members, thank you for the opportunity to testify today.

In my written testimony, I have gone into detail about Russian President Vladimir Putin's strategic objectives in the Middle East and how those work against our own national security interests. But for the sake of brevity, let me summarize.

First, Vladimir Putin's intervention in Syria in September 2015 had taken many by surprise, but it is important to remember that Russia's presence in the Middle East is not new. It is its absence during Boris Yeltsin's Presidency in the 1990 that is the deviation from history. Putin sought to bring Russia back to the Middle East from the very beginning when he officially came to power in May 2000, and he did so in an anti-Western zero-sum approach. For Putin to win, the United States had to lose.

In the Middle East, and especially in Syria, Putin has multiple goals, but fundamentally, Putin's priority is the survival of his own regime. He wants to stay in power. And survival for him is connected to undermining the West. Thus, Putin uses the Middle East to that end. He steps into vacuums wherever the West retreats and asserts Russia's influence, which sows instability and contributes to terrorism.

Putin says he wants to work with everyone in the region, but his actions show a clear preference for the anti-Sunni and anti-U.S. forces. Putin's growing relationship with Iran and continued support pursuing President Bashar al-Assad, two major forces that contribute to terrorism, are a testament to this.

Russia's growing alliance with Iran, in particular, presents a major challenge to U.S. interests in the region. We increasingly talk about a post-ISIS environment, and it is in a post-ISIS environment that this issue becomes especially important. Russia-Iran military ties continue to grow and, frankly, the overall level of closeness between the two countries is unprecedented in the grand scope of over 500 years of history.

Together, Moscow and Tehran are in a better position to undermine the U.S. in the Middle East than on their own. For years, Moscow consistently worked to dilute sanctions against Iran and claimed that concerns about Iran's nuclear program were overblown. Moscow also, at the very least, looked the other way when Russian weapons reached Hezbollah. And as was mentioned previously, Hezbollah is not designated as a terrorist organization in Russia.

Kremlin's actions shows that Putin cares more about his own interests than international regional security. In Syria, Putin protected Bashar al-Assad from the very beginning and in multiple ways. Putin says he went into Syria in September 2015 to fight terrorists, mainly ISIS, so that they don't return to Russia. But as was mentioned several times here today, numerous reports indicate that he has primarily targeted everyone else.

Putin wants to put the U.S. in front of a choice: It is either ISIS or Assad. And as Putin enables Assad, Assad continues an ethnic cleansing in Syria, which increases refugee flows into Europe, thus helping Putin weaken and divide the West.

Russia's role in Libya is particularly important to watch. Putin has been gaining a foothold there by supporting Libya's General Khalifa Haftar. And in the context of U.S. absence, Putin could attempt to do in Libya what he has effectively done in Syria, step into a vacuum, create a short-term fix, and take credit for it and cede long-term instability.

The line between domestic and foreign policy in Russia is often blurred, and it is hard sometimes to understand because it is different from the West. It is a point that often gets missed. Putin seeks to distract Russia's domestic audience from his own failings. His foreign adventures, pointing to the U.S. as the enemy, these are all distractions in many ways. This is how he legitimizes his regime. Putin fears domestic protests, and he believes that the West orchestrates regime change throughout the world, be it color revolutions in the post-Soviet space, the Arab Spring, or domestic protests against Putin himself.

Moscow's overall military moves from Ukraine to Syria suggest that Putin is trying to create antiaccess/denial, the so-called A2/AD bubbles, to limit our ability to maneuver in the region. These are, essentially, ever-growing buffer zones that he is trying to create. Thus, access to warm-water ports has been especially important to Putin along with political and economic influence in the region.

I made a number of policy recommendations in my testimony, but my top few are the following: First, Putin cannot be a reliable partner in fighting terrorism. We cannot work effectively with someone who perceives us as the enemy and seeks to undermine us and who enables forces that contribute to terrorism in the region in the first place.

Second, the United States must actively engage in the Middle East, such as increase security cooperation with our partners to reassure our allies and counter Kremlin's propaganda efforts more effectively. This is the best way to limit Putin's influence.

Lastly, we have to remember that there are no quick and easy fixes, but with strategic and moral clarity, the U.S. can reclaim its leadership position in the region.

Thank you.

[The prepared statement of Ms. Borshchevskaya follows:]

Russia's Strategic Objectives in the Middle East and North Africa

Anna Borshchevskaya
Ira Weiner Fellow, The Washington Institute for Near East Policy

Testimony submitted to the House Foreign Affairs Subcommittee on the
Middle East and North Africa
June 15, 2017

Chairwoman Ros-Lehtinen, Ranking Member Deutch, Honorable Members, thank you for the opportunity to testify today regarding Russia's strategic objectives in the Middle East and North Africa. I will focus on President Vladimir Putin's efforts to return Russia to the Middle East and especially highlight Iran, Syria, and Libya, and describe how these efforts sow instability and thus hurt U.S. interests. I will also address Moscow's overall strategic aims, and what the United States could do to limit Moscow's influence, including working with our regional partners to that end.

History matters. Russian efforts to influence the Middle East and counter U.S. interests in the region predate Russia's deployment of forces to Syria in September 2015. Imperial Russia began asserting its interests in the region in the nineteenth century. Its successor the Soviet Union worked for at least half a century to bolster its influence in the region and stymie that of the United States and its allies. It was only during Boris Yeltsin's presidency in the 1990s that Russia briefly retreated from the Middle East.

Vladimir Putin chartered Russia's return to the Middle East immediately upon assuming the presidency in May 2000. He did so in the context of zero-sum anti-Westernism -- for Russia to win, the United States had to lose. Putin's policies have roots in the vision of Yevgeny Primakov, foreign minister in 1996-1998 and subsequently prime minister in 1998-1999. Primakov was a skilled Arabist who sought a tougher, more anti-Western posture than Yeltsin was willing to embrace. Russian officials echo Primakov when they talk of a "multipolar world."[1]

Putin himself wanted to restore Russia's superpower status. He wanted the United States to recognize Russia as an equal without which Washington could make no major international decision. In the Middle East, he did so by regaining political, diplomatic, and economic influence, using increased cooperation and diplomatic exchanges, arms and energy sales, and provision of high-technology goods such as nuclear reactors. Indeed, Russia's January 2000 Foreign Policy Concept defined Moscow's priorities in the Middle East as "to restore and strengthen [Russia's] positions, particularly economic ones," and highlighted the importance of continuing to develop ties with Iran. The document highlights "attempts to

---

[1] Jonathan Steele, "Yevgeny Primakov, Obituary," *Guardian*, June 28, 2015,
https://www.theguardian.com/world/2015/jun/28/yevgeny-primakov

create an international relations structure based on domination by developed Western countries in the international community, under U.S. leadership," while asserting that NATO expansionism was among the major threats facing Russia.[2] Putin's intervention in Syria may have taken the world by surprise, but it was years in the making, and the seeds of what was to come were there from the very beginning.

Putin sought to improve ties with every regional leader, whether traditional Kremlin friend or foe. Thus, in October 2000, he publicly repealed the 1995 Gore-Chernomyrdin pact which limited Russia's sale of conventional arms to Iran. Press reports indicated that in practice the agreement gave Russia "a free pass to sell conventional weapons to Iran"[3] until 1999, but the public cancellation of the deal sent a message that Putin wanted closer cooperation with the Islamic Republic. By 2001, Iran had become the third largest buyer of Russian weaponry.[4]

Putin became the first Kremlin head of state in years to visit several Middle Eastern countries. He also received high-level Middle East officials with full honors in Moscow. For example, he visited Egypt in April 2005 -- the first such visit in forty years. In February 2007, Putin travelled to Saudi Arabia and Qatar, something no Russian -- or Soviet -- head of state had ever done.[5] Yet just as Putin offered Iran nuclear technology, he also sought business for Russia's nuclear industry in Jordan, Egypt, and the Persian Gulf, who sought to keep pace with Iran. Other high-level official exchanges between Russian and Middle Eastern officials also increased. Russia's economic ties with Turkey and Egypt grew. Putin also improved Russia's relations with Israel, even as senior Kremlin officials hosted Hamas in Moscow.[6]

By 2010, Russia had succeeded in restoring much of its Middle East influence -- including "good relations with every government and most major opposition movements," according to George Mason University Professor Mark Katz.[7] The Arab Spring came soon afterward. Moscow saw the hand of the West in these uprisings (just as it did in the color revolutions in the post-Soviet space and the largest anti-Putin protests since the end of the Cold war in late 2011-early 2012).[8] These years saw an increasingly

---

[2] Концепция национальной безопасности Российской Федерации, Russian Ministry of Foreign Affairs, January 10, 2000, http://www.mid.ru/en/foreign_policy/official_documents/-/asset_publisher/CptICkB6BZ29/content/id/589768?p_p_id=101_INSTANCE_CptICkB6BZ29&_101_INSTANCE_CptICkB6BZ29_languageId=ru_RU

[3] "Gore's Secret Pact," *Wall Street Journal*, October 18, 2000, https://www.wsj.com/articles/SB971819748452949326

[4] Ariel Cohen and James A. Phillips, "Countering Russian-Iranian Military Cooperation," Backgrounder 1425 on Russia (Heritage Foundation, April 5, 2001), http://www.heritage.org/research/reports/2001/04/counteringrussian-iranian-military-cooperation

[5] Donna Abu-Nasr, "Putin 1st Russian Leader to Visit Saudis," *Washington Post*, February 11, 2007 http://www.washingtonpost.com/wp-dyn/content/article/2007/02/11/AR2007021100048; Hassan M. Fattah, "Putin Visits Qatar for Talks on Natural Gas and Trade," *New York Times*, February 13, 2007, http://www.nytimes.com/2007/02/13/world/middleeast/13putin.html

[6] Steven Lee Myers and Greg Myer, "Hamas Delegation Visits Moscow for a Crash Course in Diplomacy," *New York Times*, March 4, 2006, http://www.nytimes.com/2006/03/04/world/04hamas.html

[7] Mark Katz, "Moscow and the Middle East: Repeat Performance?" *Russia in Global Affairs*, October 7, 2012, http://eng.globalaffairs.ru/number/Moscow-and-the-Middle-East-Repeat-Performance-15690

[8] Jonathan Steele, "Putin Still Bitter over Orange Revolution," *Guardian*, September 5, 2005, http://www.theguardian.com/world/2005/sep/06/russia.jonathansteele; Roland Oliphant, "Vladimir Putin: We Must Stop a Ukraine-Style 'Coloured Revolution' in Russia," *Telegraph*, November 20, 2014, http://www.telegraph.co.uk/news/worldnews/europe/ukraine/11243521/Vladimir-Putin-

aggressive Putin emerge as he grew insecure of his grip on power. Indeed, more recently, in December 2016, one major Kremlin-controlled publication directly described the Arab Spring as a "series of government coups in the countries of North Africa in 2011, initiated by the American special services."[9]

Russia briefly lost some influence in the Middle East during the Arab Spring, but the Kremlin successfully worked to regain much of it. For example, Putin reached out to Muslim Brotherhood leader Mohammed Morsi in Egypt, even though the Russian Supreme Court had designated the Brotherhood as a domestic terrorist organization since February 2003. Putin's outreach revealed that although he might prefer to work with secularists in Egypt, he would work with Islamists to secure Russia's influence amid the vacuum created by Western absence, even if this meant supporting an organization that in the Kremlin's own view encouraged terrorism and instability in Russia.

IRAN AND SYRIA

Over the years, the Kremlin consistently worked to dilute sanctions against Iran. Top officials frequently claimed there was no evidence that Tehran was conducting nuclear weapons research. Indeed, when the International Atomic Energy Agency announced in November 2011 that Tehran had apparently been working for years on a weapon, the Kremlin accused the agency of bias. The Russian Foreign Affairs Ministry described the report as "a compilation of well-known facts that have intentionally been given a politicized intonation."[10] Foreign Minister Sergei Lavrov has argued that Iran deserves to be an equal partner in resolving Middle East issues, and that sanctions hurt Russian-Iranian trade.[11] Moscow also at the very least looked the other way as Russian weaponry made its way into Hezbollah's hands. The Kremlin's actions show that they care more about their own interests than international or regional security.

Russia and Iran share a complicated history, but what unites them the most is their joint interest in reducing American influence, and because of this interest they have been able to put their differences aside and cooperate. Indeed, in August 2016, Moscow took the world -- and many in Iran -- by surprise when it reportedly used Iran's Hamadan airbase to bomb targets in Syria. The last time a foreign power had based itself in Iran was during World War II. In the context of public outrage in Iran, Defense Minister Hossein Dehghan accused Moscow of "ungentlemanly" behavior for publicizing its use of the base.[12] Nonetheless, Parliamentary Speaker Ali Larijani said only days afterward that "The flights [of Russian warplanes] haven't been suspended. Iran and Russia are allies in the fight against terrorism," though the

---

we-must-stop-a-Ukraine-style-coloured-revolution-in-Russia.html; "Shoigu: Scenario Based on Arab Spring Was Used in Ukraine," *RIA Novosti*, April 1, 2014, http://ria.ru/defense_safety/20140401/1002052340.html; Thomas Grove, "Russia's Putin Says the West Is on the Decline," Reuters, July 9, 2012, http://www.reuters.com/article/us-russia-putin-west-idUSBRE86818020120709

[9] "Путин: Примаков предупреждал о негативных последствиях «арабской весны»," REGNUM, December 4, 2016, https://regnum.ru/news/polit/2213257.html

[10] Ellen Barry, "Russia Dismisses Calls for New UN Sanctions on Iran," *New York Times*, November 9, 2011, http://www.nytimes.com/2011/11/10/world/europe/russia-dismisses-calls-for-new-un-sanctions-on-iran.html

[11] Michal Shmulovich, "Russia: US sanctions on Syria, Iran are hurting our businesses," *Times of Israel*, September 8, 2012, http://www.timesofisrael.com/russia-us-sanctions-in-syria-iran-are-hurting-our-businesses/

[12] Anne Barnard and Andrew E. Kramer, "Iran Revokes Russia's Use of Air Base, Saying Moscow 'Betrayed Trust,'" *New York Times*, August 22, 2016, http://www.nytimes.com/2016/08/23/world/middleeast/iran-russia-syria.html?_r=0

Hamadan air base, he claimed, was only "used for refueling."[13] And more recently, in March of this year, Foreign Minister Mohammad Javad Zarif said Russia could use Iranian military bases to launch air strikes against targets in Syria on a "case by case basis."[14] Furthermore, unlike the Sunni Muslim Brotherhood, Shia Hezbollah is not designated as a terrorist organization in Russia.

But in Syria, Russia's influence has been visible like nowhere else in the region. Putin had many interests in supporting Syrian dictator Bashar al-Assad from the very beginning -- economic, political, cultural, and geostrategic. He has armed Assad, shielded him at the UN Security Council, agreed to take Syria's crude oil in exchange for refined oil products to sustain the country's military and economy, and provided loans to stave off Syrian bankruptcy.[15] He uses the United Nations to delay meaningful action on Syria. To date, Putin continues to deny that Assad used chemical weapons against his people.[16] Putin's enabling allowed Assad to continue his ethnic cleansing policy in Syria that exacerbates refugee flows into Europe. Moscow cynically used Syria as a test case to advertise its newest weaponry and training opportunities for Russian troops, while Iran and Hezbollah learn from the Russian military.[17]

Putin also seeks access to warm-water ports. In February 2012 he renewed emphasis on improving Russia's military and in particular the navy.[18] Syria hosted Russia's only military facility outside the former Soviet Union, in Tartus. Syria also provided Putin with an opportunity to entrench Russia's military presence in the region more permanently, and gain an entry point into the region.

Putin says that he went into Syria to fight ISIS, and to kill fighters before they return to Russia.[19] But numerous reports have indicated since September 2015 that Putin's primary focus has not been on ISIS but on those fighting Assad. Moscow's actions show that its primary goal is to force the West to choose between ISIS and Assad, mainly by eliminating everyone else. If anything, Moscow is likely to increase radicalization through discriminatory policies toward Russia's own Muslims, and through enabling Assad, who himself remains the largest recruitment source for ISIS and other radical groups.

---

[13] Allen Cone, "Russia gets permission to use Iran's Hamadan air base for Syria airstrikes," UPI, November 30, 2016, http://www.upi.com/Top_News/World-News/2016/11/30/Russia-gets-permission-to-use-Irans-Hamadan-air-base-for-Syria-airstrikes/8251480520159/

[14] Vladimir Soldatkin and Kevin O'Flynn, "Iran says Russia can use its military bases 'on case by case basis,'" Reuters, March 28, 2017, http://www.reuters.com/article/us-russia-iran-rouhani-base-idUSKBN16Z0NU

[15] Anna Borshchevskaya, "Russia's Many Interests in Syria," PolicyWatch 2023, Washington Institute for Near East Policy, January 24, 2013, http://www.washingtoninstitute.org/policy-analysis/view/russias-many-interests-in-syria

[16] "Путин уверен, что Асад не применял химическое оружие," Pravda.ru, June 2, 2017, https://www.pravda.ru/news/politics/02-06-2017/1336479-siria-0/

[17] Paul Bucala and Genevieve Casagrande, "How Iran Is Learning from Russia in Syria," Understandingwar.org, February 3, 2017, http://webcache.googleusercontent.com/search?q=cache:hz51UgUkJqAJ:www.understandingwar.org/background er/how-iran-learning-russia-syria+&cd=1&hl=en&ct=clnk&gl=us; Rowan Scarborough, "Putin Using Syrian Civil War as Testing Ground for New Weapons," *Washington Times*, February 28, 2016, http://www.washingtontimes.com/news/2016/feb/28/russia-using-syria-as-testing-ground-for-new-weapo/

[18] "Владимир Путин: 'Быть сильными: гарантии национальной безопасности для России,'" *Rossiyskaya Gazeta*, February 20, 2012, https://rg.ru/2012/02/20/putin-armiya.html

[19] "Путин: ВКС РФ воюют в Сирии, чтобы в Россию не вернулись террористы," REGNUM, April 12, 2017, https://regnum.ru/news/polit/2262075.html

In March 2016, many analysts spoke positively about Russia's "withdrawal" from Syria following Putin's announcement that he was partially removing the "main part" of Russian armed forces.[20] Yet Russia never withdrew. Putin's actions showed that he was only retrenching Russia in Syria. That Russia's Hmeimim Air Base officially became permanent in October 2016, for example,[21] demonstrates the danger of taking Putin at his word.

LIBYA AND BEYOND

Moscow's foothold in Libya is growing.[22] This issue is important to watch in the months ahead. Putin increasingly supports Libya's Gen. Khalifa Haftar, who controls the oil-rich eastern part of the country but wants more. With the fall of Muammar Qadhafi in October 2011, Russia lost not only several billion dollars' worth of investments but also access to the Benghazi port.

Haftar (who served under Qadhafi) pursues an anti-Islamist agenda and looks to Putin to help secure his leadership in Libya at the expense of the UN-backed civilian government. Haftar is a deeply polarizing figure, one that by expert accounts is the wrong choice for the country. But for Putin he presents an opportunity to do what Moscow did in Syria, as U.S. Africa Command chief and Marine Corps general Thomas Waldhauser characterized the situation at a Senate Armed Services Committee hearing this March.[23] This means stepping into a vacuum left by America's absence, gaining influence and creating a short-term fix while ensuring long-term conflict and insecurity.

Russia provides the Tobruk government with military advice and diplomatic support at the UN. In May 2016, Moscow reportedly printed nearly 4 billion Libyan dinars (approximately $2.8 billion) for Libya's Central Bank and transferred the money to a branch loyal to Haftar. In the context of growing tensions with Tripoli, Haftar made two trips to Moscow in the second half of 2016, and in January of this year, he toured the Russian aircraft carrier *Admiral Kuznetsov* as it returned home from Syrian waters. While aboard the *Kuznetsov*, Haftar held a video call with Russian defense minister Sergei Shoigu and reportedly talked about fighting terrorism in the Middle East. This February, Moscow flew approximately seventy of Haftar's wounded soldiers to Russia for treatment.[24] Officially, Moscow denies any talk with Haftar about creating military bases in Libya, but it's easy to see how such a base, or at least another form of Russian military presence, would be consistent with Moscow's actions in recent years.

---

[20] "Путин приказал начать вывод основных сил РФ из Сирии с 15 марта," Tass, March 14, 2016, http://tass.ru/politika/2738218

[21] David Filipov and Andrew Roth,"Russia Has Its Permanent Air Base in Syria. Now It's Looking at Cuba and Vietnam," *Washington Post*, October 7, 2016 https://www.washingtonpost.com/news/worldviews/wp/2016/10/07/russia-has-its-permanent-airbase-in-syria-now-its-looking-at-cuba-and-vietnam/?utm_term=.f4787278dd2b

[22] Idrees Ali and Phil Stewart, "Link seen between Russia and Libyan commander Haftar: U.S. general," Reuters, March 24, 2017, http://www.reuters.com/article/us-usa-libya-russia-idUSKBN16V2IW

[23] Daniel Brown, "Lawmakers Urge US to Get Serious on Russia's Growing Influence in Libya," Business Insider, April 26, 2017, http://www.businessinsider.com/us-lawmakers-urge-action-in-libya-where-russia-has-gained-a-foothold-2017-4

[24] Ayman Al-Warfalli and Patrick Markey, "Eastern Libya forces fly wounded to Russia in growing cooperation," Reuters, February 1 2017, http://www.reuters.com/article/us-libya-security-russia-idUSKBN15G4VW

Meanwhile, Russia's ties with Egypt continue to grow, while Turkey, a NATO ally, is falling deeper into Putin's orbit than perhaps even Turkish president Recep Tayyip Erdogan himself may realize. That Turkey came to accept Russia's position on Assad in Syria, for instance, is a testament to Moscow's influence. Russia's deep ties to the Kurds that go back at least two centuries are among the key reasons why Putin has leverage over Erdogan.

MOSCOW'S LARGER STRATEGIC OBJECTIVES

The line between domestic and foreign policies is blurred in Russia to a degree that can be difficult to understand in the West.[25] Moscow's aggressive foreign policy often coincides with domestic problems. Prominent Russian satirist Mikhail Saltykov-Shchedrin once remarked, "They [the powers that be] are talking a lot about patriotism -- must have stolen again."[26] And Vyacheslav Plehve, the czar's interior minister, famously suggested in 1904 that what Russia needs is a "short, victorious war to stem the flow of revolution."[27]

Putin fears domestic protest. It was no accident this March when he compared the recent wave of anti-corruption protests in Russia to the Arab Spring and Euromaidan,[28] both of which he believes were orchestrated by the West. From a traditional Western standpoint, it is the rising powers that are most worrisome, but when it comes to Russia, it is weakness that should worry the West. Putin feels that if he doesn't protect his interests in the Middle East, he himself is next. Putin also feels that America's talk of democracy is not real, but pretext for regime change.[29] He believes this because if the situation were reversed, that is what he would do.

Taken as a whole, Putin's military moves are about creating and extending virtual buffer zones along Russia's periphery through antiaccess/area-denial bubbles in order to limit the West's ability to maneuver. Such moves are not new. For centuries, the Kremlin felt that Russia's expansion necessitated buffer zones in a self-perpetuating cycle: the more lands Moscow gained, the more insecure it felt when faced with the challenges of administering remote territories, and the more buffers it sought.[30]

---

[25] Bobo Lo, *Russia and the New World Disorder* (London: Brookings Institution Press with Chatham House, 2015), pp. 24-25.

[26] As quoted in Leon Aaron, "Why Vladimir Putin Says Russia Is Exceptional," *Wall Street Journal*, May 30, 2014, https://www.wsj.com/articles/why-putin-says-russia-is-exceptional-1401473667

[27] As quoted in Anders Aslund, "Russia Will Pay Dearly for Putin's Anschluss," *Moscow Times*, March 25, 2014, https://piie.com/commentary/op-eds/russia-will-pay-dearly-putins-anschluss

[28] "Путин сравнил митинги в России с началом «арабской весны» и «Евромайдана,» " *Republic*, March 30, 2017, https://republic.ru/posts/81313

[29] Putin routinely justified his own actions by comparing them to what he perceived as similar U.S. actions. For example, he reportedly defended his control of the Russian media by saying, "Don't lecture me about the free press, not after you fired that reporter," referring to CBS Evening News anchor Dan Rather, who was stepping down after his report on George W. Bush's National Guard service turned out to be fraudulent. See Peter Baker, "The Seduction of George W. Bush," *Foreign Policy*, November 6, 2013, http://foreignpolicy.com/2013/11/06/the-seduction-of-george-w-bush/

[30] Anders Aslund and Andy Kuchins, *The Russia Balance Sheet* (Peterson Institute for International Economics, 2009), p. 12.

At the same time, as last year's NATO Defense College report indicated, Russia's weakness should not be confused with fragility; Putin's Russia retains certain strengths.[31] In the Middle East, Putin's increasingly warm ties with Iran -- and more broadly anti-Sunni forces -- also put him in a better position to confront the United States in the Middle East than he would have been able to alone. Putin certainly wants to maintain ties with everyone in the region, but at the same time his actions clearly show a preference for the Shia axis.

POLICY RECOMMENDATIONS

If Washington wants to limit Moscow's influence and improve the U.S. strategic position vis-a-vis Russia in the Middle East and North Africa, it should embrace a strategy that includes the following:

- **Recognize Putin is no partner to fight terrorism.** While fighting terrorism is in Russia's interest, Putin's actions show that he is more interested in undermining and dividing the West than working with it. This includes empowering forces in Tehran and Damascus that are responsible for terrorism. Furthermore, Putin needs the West as a foil upon whom he can blame his own domestic failings. Therefore, U.S. officials should limit contact with Putin to military deconfliction. Conciliation will backfire. Putin responds productively only when American officials act from a position of strength.

- **Engage actively in the Middle East.** Russia need not be America's military or economic equal to pose a challenge to Western interests. For example, Russia has only one aircraft carrier, *Admiral Kuznetsov*; it is rusty, leaky, and prone to fire. The United States meanwhile has ten far more advanced carriers. Yet by simply being present when the United States was absent, Putin has complicated the operating environment in the Middle East and Mediterranean and augmented Russia's influence.

- **Improve security cooperation.** The U.S. Navy could increase port visits in the Eastern Mediterranean and Middle East to reinforce the notion within the region that America supports and defends allies and is not in retreat.[32] The military could also augment exercises beyond those it conducts annually with Morocco, Egypt, and Jordan, emphasizing interoperability among pro-Western Arab states.

- **Engage militarily in Syria.** For years Putin perceived weakness from the West, asserting himself in Syria because he believed the West would do nothing in response. Policymakers deterred themselves into inaction in Syria because they worried about a military confrontation with Russia. Yet Putin understands his limitations, and a direct confrontation is not something he seeks. Indeed, as the April 7 U.S. cruise missile strikes showed, for all of the Kremlin's bluster, in the

---

[31] Richard Connolly, *Towards Self Sufficiency? Economics as a Dimension of Russian Security and the National Security Strategy of the Russian Federation to 2020*, NATO Defense College, July 18, 2016, http://www.ndc.nato.int/news/news.php?icode=964

[32] Anna Borshchevskaya and Cmdr. Jeremy Vaughan, USN , "How The Russian Military Reestablished Itself in the Middle East," PolicyWatch 2709, Washington Institute for Near East Policy, October 17, 2016, http://www.washingtoninstitute.org/policy-analysis/view/how-the-russian-military-reestablished-itself-in-the-middle-east

end it could do nothing but complain. Rather than provoking conflict with Russia, for the first time in years Putin received a message that the United States had redlines he and his proxies could not cross. Therefore, instead, of enticing Putin with incentives, Washington should demonstrate that his embrace of Assad brings tremendous costs to Russia.

- **Target diplomacy.** Military strategy alone will not deliver. It is essential not only to resource U.S. diplomacy, but also to direct diplomats to actively counter Russian moves in the region. Funding itself is not a metric for effectiveness absent a broader strategy.

- **Invest more resources in countering the Kremlin's propaganda efforts.** Russian propaganda seeks to confuse, sow doubt, and ultimately create paralysis. Lies don't need to last in order to do lasting damage. In the Middle East, Russian propaganda fuels conspiracy thinking, feeding on the region's existing proclivities. Rather than always being on the defensive, the United States should work harder at creating first impressions. As a recent RAND study indicates, according to psychologists, first impressions remain highly resilient, and because Russian propaganda is not concerned with the truth, it often holds the monopoly on them.[33] Here the United States can work with regional partners to establish outlets that provide alternative sources of information and counter Moscow's negative influence.

- **Recognize there is no easy fix and settle in for the long haul.** We often talk about Putin being a short-term thinker. But he has been in power now for seventeen years and does not have to constrain himself to the limited political timelines under which democratic leaders operate. Putin's Achilles heel is exposed when U.S. policymakers reclaim leadership with moral clarity.

---

[33] Christopher Paul and Miriam Matthews, *The Russian "Firehose of Falsehood" Propaganda Model: Why It Might Work and Options to Counter It* (Santa Monica, CA: RAND Corporation, 2016), https://www.rand.org/pubs/perspectives/PE198.html

23

Mr. Donovan [presiding]. Thank you.
Our next witness.

STATEMENT OF MR. BRIAN KATULIS, SENIOR FELLOW, CENTER FOR AMERICAN PROGRESS

Mr. Katulis. Great. I would like to thank the acting chairman and the ranking member and all members of the committee for the invitation. It is great to be with you today.

My bottom line analysis upfront is that Russia's increased engagement and assertiveness in the Middle East since 2015 has accelerated three negative trends within the region that affect U.S. national security interests.

One is it has accelerated State fragmentation; two, it has actually heightened the terrorist threat posed in the region and to the United States; and three, it has reinforced a trend toward autocratic and authoritarian rule. It has done this primarily through its longstanding cooperation with Iran, but its backing most recently of the Assad regime in Syria.

Another bottom line upfront assessment is that though it is still too early to tell in the Trump administration, I believe that we are seeing the emergence of a strategic posture of the United States in the Middle East that is quite incoherent and not clear where the pieces do not add up.

I would like to use my remarks to talk, first, for a minute about the strategic landscape in the Middle East, because I think it is very important to stress one key point: That the region itself is in the midst of a long and complicated period of fluid change, and the drivers of that change largely come from within the region. Outside actors like the United States, like Russia, have an important sway and influence, but the primary drivers of change inside the region come from within the actors.

Some of it is this competition for influence between Saudi Arabia and Iran. Some of it are these tensions we have seen recently between other major actors like Qatar and other Gulf States. And a big part of it is this rise of nonstate actors that we have seen over the last 15 to 20 years, including al-Qaeda and the Islamic State.

This competition within the region is multidimensional. It has a military and security aspect, but it has political and economic features that I am happy to talk about. It is multipolar, meaning that there is not one single actor or force that I see as dominant within the region. So I think this complicated landscape is one that is subject to fracturing, fragmentation, and every action the United States takes, every action outside actors like Russia takes, it makes a major impact, and it is quite vulnerable.

In my written testimony, I outline seven key objectives that I see in Russia's behaviors in the Middle East. I would like to just highlight a few and then move to my assessment of U.S. policy.

Number one, it is clear to me that Russia and its actions, particularly since 2015, have been aimed to safeguard against attempts to isolate Russia geopolitically for its destabilizing actions in Europe, in Ukraine, in the United States, and other parts of the world. Part of the reason I think it got engaged was not only to try to undermine U.S. influence in the region, but also to, again, arrest the attempts to isolate it through various means.

Secondly, it has tried to maintain a degree of military presence at strategic locations across the Middle East and North Africa, primarily, we see in eastern Mediterranean and Syria.

And then, lastly, it states that it seeks to contain Islamist terrorism and prevent its expansion into Russia and its own borders. But, again, if you go back to my bottom line assessment, the consequence of its actions have been to exacerbate and to worsen that threat.

In my last minute, I just wanted to briefly talk about what I see as very worrisome trends, and I think an important role that Congress has to play in asking questions. We have moved from a policy in the previous decade under the Bush administration of, perhaps, overreach and trying to do so much to change these societies to one under President Obama of reticence and restraint, to what I think at this stage, 5 months into a new administration, which is quite incoherent at this point. The pieces don't add up.

Three points I would stress in the emerging strategic posture in the Trump administration and why I think it is important that you are having this hearing and Congress should engage on these issues:

Number one, we see a proposed unilateral disarmament of the tools of U.S. national security power, particularly in diplomacy and economic tools. And that is why this bill that several of the members talked about that is in the Senate, I think is an important tool in the arsenal to shape the actions of Russia and Iran in ways that benefit our interests. Secondly, we see an overreliance on military tactics in the absence of a clear strategy. And thirdly, I also see what I term a creeping U.S. military escalation and a silent surge of U.S. troops in multiple parts of the Middle East, in Syria and Yemen and other places, but all of this is in absence of overarching strategy.

What is the best way to deal with Russia in the Middle East? The best and most effective thing is to have a coherent U.S. strategy, something that I would submit that we have not had for more than a decade and a half. In large part because of our own unforced errors, in large part because of this complicated landscape I tried to depict in my written testimony and in my remarks today. But Congress has an important role in helping this new administration find greater coherence and develop greater coherence in its engagement strategy.

Thank you very much.

[The prepared statement of Mr. Katulis follows:]

Center for American Progress

1333 H Street, NW, 10ᵗʰ Floor
Washington, DC 20005
Tel: 202.682.1611 • Fax: 202.682.1867

www.americanprogress.org

Assessing the Impact of Russia's Support for Authoritarian State Sponsors of Terrorism in the Middle East and North Africa

Brian Katulis
Senior Fellow
Center for American Progress
June 15, 2017

Testimony Before the House Foreign Affairs Subcommittee on the Middle East and North Africa on Russia's Strategic Objectives in the Middle East and North Africa

Chairman Ros-Lehtinen, Ranking Member Deutch, and members of the committee, thank you for the opportunity to appear before you today to discuss Russia's strategic objectives in the Middle East and North Africa. I have structured my testimony today around three main points:

1. An overview of the current strategic landscape in the Middle East and North Africa

2. An assessment of Russia's objectives in the Middle East and North Africa

3. An initial analysis of the new U.S. administration's emerging strategic posture in the Middle East and North Africa and how it is likely to impact Russian policies in the region.

My bottom line assessment is that Russia's increased engagement in the Middle East has accelerated the ongoing trends towards state fragmentation, heightened terrorism, and ongoing displacement in key parts of the region, while also reinforcing autocratic tendencies of key powers in the region. In particular, Russia's support for the Assad regime in Syria and cooperation with Iran undercuts U.S. strategic objectives.

Strategic Landscape in the Middle East and North Africa in Early 2017

The starting point for analyzing Russia's objectives in the Middle East and North Africa is an examination of the current landscape in the region.

The broader Middle East and North Africa remains embroiled in an uncertain and fluid period of change. This change is largely driven by factors within the region. It involves a heightened competition for influence among key countries such as Saudi Arabia and

Iran, the fragility of states such as Yemen and Syria produced by a crisis of political legitimacy, and the growing power of non-state actors – especially terrorist groups such as Al Qaeda, the Islamic State, and Hezbollah. Outside actors such as the United States, Russia, European countries, and China have demonstrated a capacity to shape and influence trends, but the main drivers come from within the region.

The leading state powers within the region are engaged in a complicated, multidimensional, and multipolar struggle for influence and power. This struggle is multidimensional because key actors in the region use a wide range of tools to assert their interests. In some instances, the countries of the region engage in proxy wars, such as Yemen, where Saudi Arabia and Iran have offered support to different forces inside the country. Regional powers also use traditional forms of power projection – military aid and economic assistance – to expand their influence.

But increasingly, governments and non-state actors in the region use new tools of power to advance their agendas, including direct investments in media and disinformation campaigns that target other countries and political actors and work to alter domestic power balances within them. The ongoing tension within the Gulf Cooperation Council countries involving Qatar is the latest episode in a larger battle for influence involving many countries in the region. This unresolved situation risks a strategic shift that draws countries such as Qatar and Turkey closer to Iran.

This competition for power and influence in the Middle East today is multipolar and unlikely to produce a single hegemon or dominant power within the region. Sunni-Shia sectarian divisions offer only a partial description of what is happening inside of the Middle East. Recent tensions between the different countries of the Gulf Cooperation Council, Turkey, and Egypt, for instance, involve countries with Sunni Muslim majority populations. Moreover, Israel has for the most part worked to preserve its own security by seeking quiet, tactical cooperation with as many Sunni-majority countries in the Middle East to counter Iran. All in all, this broader landscape presents few opportunities for sustainable security.

The multipolar and multidimensional struggle for influence is likely to continue for the foreseeable future, and it will likely continue to strain the overall state system of the Middle East. Like balls in a game of billiards, countries in the Middle East crash into each other and veer off in unexpected directions. In this game of billiards, though, some of the balls are weak and fracture on contact. Military actions against terrorist groups such as ISIS will continue to inflict damage on these groups. But without an overall strategy that integrates all aspects of power these actions may not lead to their lasting defeat – and in fact could produce even more conflict, state fragmentation, and a next generation of terrorist networks.

Within this context, Russia has stepped up its engagement in the Middle East since 2015 in a manner that boosted authoritarian state sponsors of terrorism in the region. These moves have benefited Russia to a degree – in particular, arresting its slide towards broader geostrategic isolation, - but they have yet to yield major strategic gains. How the

United States responds to Russia's actions in the Middle East and North Africa can help shape the trends towards authoritarianism in the region and the continued fight against the evolving terrorist threats from within the region.

Assessment of Russia's Objectives in the Middle East and North Africa

Overall, the Middle East and North Africa is a lower priority for Russia's national security strategy compared with its relations with the United States, Europe, China, and Asia. For more than two decades starting in the early 1990s, Russia had not heavily invested in building relationships across the Middle East and North Africa.

But in 2015, Russia's entry into Syria's civil war and its increased diplomatic outreach to several authoritarian state sponsors and incubators of terrorism such as Iran, Syria, and Turkey made it a more relevant force in the Middle East and North Africa. Despite its internal political, economic, and social weaknesses (as witnessed by its recent and continued domestic unrest), Russia has been able to have greater impact in the Middle East and North Africa than many analysts would have predicted two years ago.

Russia's objectives in the Middle East and North Africa include:

1. To safeguard against attempts to isolate Russia geopolitically for its destabilizing actions in Ukraine, Europe, the United States, and other parts of the world.

2. To check and undermine the influence of the United States and its NATO allies across the region.

3. To support regimes in the Middle East that are willing to cooperate with Russia.

4. To maintain a degree of Russian military presence at strategic locations across the Middle East and North Africa.

5. To contain Islamist terrorism and prevent its expansion into Russia and its immediate neighborhood.

6. To expand Russian commercial ties and build markets for Russian arms, nuclear power, and other products;

7. To coordinate energy policy with oil and gas producers in the Gulf region.

During the course of the past two years, Russia has taken actions to advance these objectives in a way that has enhanced the power and position of authoritarian governments, particularly Syria and Iran. Although Russia's strategic communications regularly highlights that it seeks to counter terrorist groups, the reality is that Russia has cooperated closely with leading state sponsors and incubators of terrorism, worsening Middle East stability.

Russia's most dramatic move was its military entry into Syria's civil war in September 2015. This intervention prolonged the fighting inside of the country, aided and abetted the killings of thousands of civilians, increased refugee flows, and contributed to a worsening humanitarian situation. Recent diplomatic efforts between Russia, Turkey, and Iran to produce a cessation of hostilities are unlikely to result in a sustainable peace due to the fragmented nature of the conflict and their reliance on terrorist organizations and state sponsors of terrorism to produce stability.

Russia's enduring cooperation with Iran, a top state sponsor and incubator of terrorism, is also serious cause for concern to the United States. Moscow's economic interests in Iran have included helping Iran develop nuclear power reactors and supplying passenger airplanes, among other industries. Russia has also provided considerable arms to Iran, including air defense systems, combat aircraft, submarines, T-72 tanks, armored personnel carriers, and other combat vehicles. Talk of Russia making a strategic break from Iran appears unrealistic.

More broadly in the Middle East and North Africa, Russia has moved to create a network of partners in Egypt, Libya, and parts of the Arab Gulf. It has also sought to coordinate policy with Israel as Israel works to secure its territory from the cauldron of threats along its borders.

The sum total of Russia's efforts since 2015 has been to reinforce the two negative trends harmful long-term U.S. strategic interests across the region: the evolution of terrorist threats and increased authoritarianism. Russia's alignment with Iran and Syria is exhibit one. But Russia's growing ties with Turkey and Egypt also show the trend towards offering support to authoritarian governments that may incubate terrorism through their actions and have not exhibited a capacity to effectively deal with the evolving terrorist threat in the region.

Assessment of the New U.S. Administration's Emerging Middle East Strategy

Compared to the recent footholds Russia has been able to establish across the region, the United States has a broader and deeper network of relationships with a wider array of regional actors than Russia. Moreover, the United States possesses greater capacities to influence these actors than Russia. Accordingly, the United States remains the main strategic partner of choice for many countries in the region.

What the United States possesses in the traditional military and economic measures of power is hampered by the lack of a coherent strategic approach to the broader Middle East and North Africa. For more than a decade and a half, the United States has lacked a coherent strategic approach to the broader region in the wake of the invasion of Iraq and the end of the policy of dual containment of both Iraq and Iran in 2003. The Bush administration's global war on terrorism and freedom agenda led to the 2003 Iraq war, and this contributed to the strategic disarray of U.S. policy in the Middle East. The Obama administration reacted by seeking to limit America's overall exposure to the

Middle East and its complicated internal dynamics, but this repositioning did not produce substantial gains in the fight against terrorists and the struggle for stability in the Middle East and North Africa.

It is too soon to assess the trajectory of the Trump administration's nascent strategy for the Middle East and North Africa. In just under five months, the Trump administration has sought to reassure partners in the region and address the trust deficit that had emerged over the past two U.S. administrations between the United States and key regional partners such as Israel, Egypt, and Saudi Arabia. However, these overtures have forsaken – if not outright disavowed – the long-standing U.S. concerns over human rights, political repression, and economic reform that past administrations viewed as drivers of instability and even extremism.

It is also premature to assess how the Trump administration's Middle East and North Africa policy will respond to Russia's renewed assertiveness in the region. The administration's emerging overall strategic approach of the Trump administration appears to lead the United States towards an overdependence on military tools while proposing drastic diminution of U.S. diplomacy through budget cuts and key diplomatic and national security posts left unfilled. But how the Trump administration will seek to work with Russia in places like Syria remains unclear and will be determined in large part by ongoing discussions on ending Syria's conflict.

In this context, the United States should take three steps to more effectively advance its interests. First, it would be prudent for the United States to add more tools to its foreign policy and national security toolbox in order to counter Russia's coordination with key state sponsors and incubators of terrorism in the Middle East. It would also be wise for the United States to invest in the complete arsenal of national security tools, particularly diplomacy and economic engagement tools aimed at influencing behaviors of countries like Russia, Syria and Iran.

Second, Congress should examine any proposed weapons sales like additional arms to Saudi Arabia and military assistance to countries like Egypt very carefully and ask tough questions to the Trump administration and America's partners in the region. The central question is how this security cooperation will produce greater stability and result in de-escalation, rather than the continued fragmentation of the state system in the Middle East. Another key question is determining what impact these weapons have on Russia's strategy in the Middle East and North Africa.

Lastly, Congress should renew the debate on a new authorization for the use of military force and raise questions about the creeping U.S. military escalation in key parts of the Middle East and North Africa. The number of U.S. troops operating closer to the frontlines of key conflicts including Syria has increased over the past year, and it essential that the new U.S. administration clarify its overall strategy for the region.

———————

Mr. DONOVAN. Thank you very much.

I thank all of our witnesses for appearing today and for their testimony.

My colleague, Ann Wagner, has to be at a markup in Financial Services, so I am going to yield my time and recognize Mrs. Wagner.

Mrs. WAGNER. Well, I thank the chair very, very much for his indulgence and generosity there. And I thank us all for participating in this important hearing, especially our witnesses today.

It is important that the committee actively tracks Russia's military partnerships and military sales in the Middle East and in North Africa.

Mr. Kara-Murza—and I hope I am getting everyone's pronunciations correct today—you are, sir, a brave supporter of Russia's democratic opposition and shoulder great personal risk, sir. I read an interview with you in the National Review and was blown away by your insight into Putin and obstacles to democracy in Russia. I appreciate your leadership. I associate myself with your stubbornness and your willingness to be here today.

I am wondering if you could flush out for us, on the record, the difference between Russia's perspective on Ukraine and the Baltic States? What about Ukraine poses a threat to Putin in a way that the Baltics do not?

Mr. KARA-MURZA. Thank you very much. Make sure the mic is on.

Thank you, Madam Congresswoman, and thank you for your very kind words. Far too kind. Again, it is an honor for me to be here.

And it is a very important question that you pose, and there is actually, a qualitative and substantive difference, I think, between Mr. Putin's perception of what is happening, for example, in the Baltic States and what is happening in the Ukraine.

Successful democratic European Baltic States would not necessarily be a direct example for Russian society, because we are so different in many ways. A successful democratic European Ukraine would be an inspiration to so many people in Russia, because of our proximity, we have, in many ways, a shared history. We have the same faith. We have a very similar language, many cultural links. And when Mr. Putin saw those images of the Maidan in Ukraine in 2013 and 2014, when he saw hundreds of thousands of people standing on the streets of the capital as the corrupt authoritarian leader, Mr. Yanukovych, was hastily getting in his helicopter and fleeing, that was an analogy too close to home for Vladimir Putin. That was not a precedent he enjoyed.

He feared that a success of this experiment, of the democratic experiment in Ukraine, would provide an inspiration for many people in Russia. And I think the primary motivation for Vladimir Putin's aggression against Ukraine for what he has been doing to Ukraine since 2014 has been the desire to prevent the success of the Maidan in Kiev before it would become a model for Maidan in Moscow.

Mrs. WAGNER. Thank you very much. And I concur.

Ms. Borshchevskaya, you have written extensively on the Putin-Erdogan relationship. Do you believe that Erdogan's decision to no longer voice support for the ousting of Assad is related to Turkey's partnership with Russia in the Syrian war? And further to that, how has Russia's historic support for the Kurdistan Workers Party, PKK, in Turkey altered how Erdogan approaches the Syrian war?

Ms. BORSHCHEVSKAYA. Thank you for the question. Yes, I believe that is exactly the reason why Erdogan has changed his mind. Frankly, I am not sure if Erdogan is realizing how unequal the relationship is right now between himself and Putin, precisely for the reason that you mentioned, because Russia has longstanding, very deep ties to Kurds. The PKK, essentially, was created by a communist proxy, and Moscow's ties to the Kurds go back over 200 years.

This is what Erdogan fears the most. And I think he, essentially, changed his position on Assad. He said for years Assad must go. He no longer says this in exchange for his ability to at least have some sort of influence in Syria.

Mrs. WAGNER. In my brief time left, Russian Ambassador to Turkey, Andrey Karlov, was fatally shot in December in Turkey. And at the time, Russia and Turkey stated that the murder was a result of terrorism. And one Russian center said that the answer would be to redouble the fight against terrorism in Syria.

Ms. Borshchevskaya, can you explain how Russia has directly or indirectly reacted to the murder in the months since then?

Ms. BORSHCHEVSKAYA. Well, for one thing—you know, the first thing that came out in the Russian Kremlin-controlled press that I remember, was talk about how these are—the murder, that these are all—it is a plot to divide Erdogan and Putin, that there is some kind of conspiracy theory. And, therefore, Erdogan and Putin are just going to keep working together more closely, that they are not going to let these fictitious enemies, these terrorists, keep them apart.

You know, beyond that, there was a very general statement about terrorism, but again, as we have talked before, these are not real attempts to fight terrorism.

Mrs. WAGNER. Thank you. And I know my time has lapsed. I yield back, and again, appreciate the indulgence of the chair.

Mr. DONOVAN. Thank you, Mrs. Wagner.

The chair now recognizes the gentleman from Florida, Mr. Deutch.

Mr. DEUTCH. Thank you, Mr. Chairman.

And thanks, again, to the witnesses for really excellent testimony. We appreciate you being here.

I would like to start with the point I made in my opening remarks, which gets to the fundamental difference in Russia's approach to the region, and that is the interview the Russian Ambassador to Israel gave just this week where he made very clear that Russia does not view ISIS the same way it views Hezbollah. And according to translations of the interview he said, "You equate ISIS with Hamas and Hezbollah, but we think this is wrong."

When pressed by the interviewer with, that is all you can say, there are bad terrorists and good terrorists, his response was, "No, we do not consider them to be terrorists at all."

So it is no wonder that Russia has had no problem aligning itself with Hezbollah in Syria and Iran, the largest state sponsor of terrorism.

Russia's interests in Syria are about making sure Russia isn't affected by ISIS, and if it means propping up a brutal dictator or empowering a different terrorist organization, one that it sees as less of a threat to its own territory, that seems to be just fine.

Apparently, Russia should be reminded that Hezbollah has launched attacks in Europe or that Hezbollah has 120,000 rockets aimed at Israel where more than 1 million Russians live. This is precisely the reason that when our President says he wants to work with Russia to fight ISIS, we have deep concerns.

I, frankly, see no outcome in which Russia suddenly separates itself from the Assad-Iran-Hezbollah alliance. And any deal that leaves a permanent Hezbollah or Iranian presence in Syria should be unacceptable to the United States. A sustained military presence in Syria would pose a serious threat to our interests in the region and only serve to further ferment Iran's destabilizing behaviors throughout the region.

So I would ask the panel, what is Russia's relationship like with Hezbollah on the battlefield, and to what extent are they cooperating and coordinating with Hezbollah, Iran, or other Iranian-backed militias?

Ms. Borshchevskaya.

Ms. BORSHCHEVSKAYA. Sure. I can address this. Sorry. There have been multiple reports that Hezbollah has been learning from the Russian military. They have—and Putin, actually, has made it no secret. He repeatedly said that the Syria campaign provided direct life training for the Russian military, and this was one among many objectives. He said, you know, that there is no better training than real-life combat. And, in fact, the Russian military already had three such campaigns in the last several years: Georgia, Ukraine, and now Syria.

So with respect to Iran and Hezbollah, you know, if you look at what is happening in Syria right now, on the Syria-Iraq border, as you know, it was reported in the press that U.S., in fact, is getting more involved. There were some clashes with pro-Assad forces. What was happening there is Russia was providing air cover for Hezbollah operations. So from reports that we have seen, there's been a lot of learning, and Hezbollah members even talked positively about how much they have learned from watching the Russians operate.

Mr. DEUTCH. Mr. Katulis?

Mr. KATULIS. If I could underscore a point, Congressman, that you stressed. Hezbollah is our adversary. It is an enemy. It has threatened, as recently as last week, U.S. troops in southern Syria, as Anna just highlighted. There were clashes. And I talked about a creeping military escalation and a silencer to the U.S. troops. We don't have the large numbers of troops that we had in Iraq and Afghanistan, thank heavens, in the previous decade, but we do have a garrison in southeastern Syria that, just last week, was threatened by Hezbollah.

So the strategic incoherence that I simply do not understand and I think Congress needs to ask tough questions of the Trump administration of how are you going to work with Russia, which has been in alignment with Iran, which is an adversary to Israel? And nobody, I think, has answered that question in any clear way, especially while Hezbollahis threatening our troops.

Mr. DEUTCH. And just if you could be—if you could be very direct, the result of a Russian-trained Hezbollah force in a post-conflict Syria with Hezbollah remaining in place means what to U.S. troops and to our—and to our ally Israel?

Mr. KATULIS. Well, to our ally Israel, when I go to Israel, they talk about Iran being their deepest strategic threat, so this approach is existential. And if I might add, when I look at the Trump administration's budget proposal for 2018 and things that it proposes to do in terms of cutting security assistance to some of those partners, including in Lebanon, that are fighting Hezbollah and its influence, it seems to me that the Trump administration has an incoherent formula that is going soft on Hezbollah, and it is perplexing.

Mr. DEUTCH. Thank you.

Mr. Chairman, the incoherent formula Mr. Katulis describes that is not only going soft on Hezbollah but helping to train Hezbollah imperils our own troops and imperils Israel, and the administration has to acknowledge as much and the policy has to change. That is why this hearing is so important.

I appreciate the opportunity. And I apologize, I am a ranking member on another committee that I have to run to, but I thank you for your time, Mr. Chairman.

Mr. DONOVAN. The chair now recognizes the gentleman from California, Mr. Rohrabacher.

Mr. ROHRABACHER. Before my friend leaves, let me just note that perhaps you have forgotten that Assad has had three decades of a truce with Israel. And let me add that, during that time, we were allied with countries that wanted to destroy Israel, our now Saudi new friends. I just wanted to—in your last statement—yes, please.

Mr. DEUTCH. Would the gentleman yield?

I mean, if the gentleman—if my friend from California is suggesting that somehow it is in the best interest of the United States to not only accept but encourage a Syria run by a brutal dictator propped up by a Russian Government——

Mr. ROHRABACHER. That is not what my statement was.

Mr. DEUTCH [continuing]. Propped up by a Russian Government that will simultaneously strengthen Hezbollah and Iran, who is an existential threat to Israel——

Mr. ROHRABACHER. That is not my——

Mr. DEUTCH [continuing]. I would disagree with that, and I——

Mr. ROHRABACHER. Okay. Well, that is the way to dodge my point, but you are absolutely wrong in your analysis that Assad, over these last 30 years, has been some kind of enemy of Israel. The fact is, we have been supporting enemies of Israel for the last 30 years. Assad is at a truce, the one country where they could have had a truce, and—I have given you your chance. Okay. You didn't answer—you didn't answer it.

Mr. DEUTCH [continuing]. The point is Assad is a murderous thug, though——

Mr. ROHRABACHER. Mr. Chairman, I gave him his chance to answer my disagreement. He chose not to.

The fact is that we have been allied with people who are much more warlike than Assad. And Assad, over these last 30 years, have been the one country in which Christians could come and seek refuge. Even from countries in which they were our friends, the Christians would come and seek refuge with Assad, because we—they, Assad, was not putting up with the persecution and destruction of the Christian community. Anything—that is what I mean by unrelenting hostility, but you can't see and in any way accept that or deal with it.

We are going to come up with the wrong policies, just like our friend—and I respect the open Russia movement. I respect the people that are struggling to get rid of the massive corruption that you have in that country. And I—unfortunately, I don't think you are making much headway right now. And it is not just removing Putin. It is removing a lot of other people in power, the oligarchs, et cetera.

But with that said, for you to suggest that the removal of Yanukovych in Ukraine was part of a democratic experience or experiment, ladies and gentlemen, you had a democratically elected government removed by force. And without that happening, I believe that Yanukovych would have been removed overwhelmingly in the next election. And collusion with Europe and the United States, powerful forces in the Ukraine, overthrew the Yanukovych regime, not allowing democracy to work; it destroyed democracy.

Mr. Chairman, I happen to be the chairman of the committee that has oversight over this part of the world, and I would never have a panel of at least some disagreement on the panel. And the bottom line is, you are about as close to any disagreement on it, and you don't.

The fact is that we need—if we are going to have peace in the world, we have got to make sure we are talking with Russia honestly and trying to confront these issues, whether it is Yanukovych or whether—you know, look, our people in the Middle East, they are not democratic countries. You think the Saudis are democratic countries? And the Saudis were involved with killing 3,000 Americans on 9/11. What about the Qataris we are talking about right now? You think they wouldn't slaughter the large populations they have, if they ever rose up against them?

We have to quit trying to judge Russia on a double standard if we want peace in this world. Because we have to reach out to them and say, okay. Let's be honest. What is in your interest? What is in our interest? I have to believe that peace is in the interest of both of our countries, especially when you have got radical Islam that is killing a bunch of Russians just like they are killing Americans.

So with that said, I will ask a question and try to get—but I am disappointed that the panel doesn't have at least one witness to try to have a dialogue about these particular issues.

By the way, just for my friend—and I am sorry he left, and I would have given him a chance to say this as well—but when you complain about any type of this administration's relationship or President, you know, Donald Trump's relationship with Russia before he was President, I mean, no one's—that doesn't sound anywhere near as insidious as the tens of millions of dollars that were put into the Clinton fund. Look, Clinton has a foundation in which oligarchs put millions and millions of dollars and paid her husband huge sums of money into his pocket. And what happened very shortly after that? Well, they get a contract to have America's uranium. My gosh. No one's even mentioning it, as if all the other stuff, talking to some—talking to an Ambassador is some sort of a secret, insidious thing, which it is not. That is what the Ambassador is there for—versus exchanges of millions of dollars? No.

We have got—if we want to have peace—I think free people should be for peace. Our major goal should be for peace because peace will override and destroy lives and destroy democracy every time. And I thank God that Ronald Reagan brought peace between Russia and the United States. He eliminated the Soviet Union. The Russians pulled back in the greatest peaceful removal of force in a large chunk of territory dealing with their borders in the history of human kind. And then what did we do? We didn't let them in the EU. We isolated them economically.

And I will just say that I played little parts in this. I mentioned the thing about trying to make sure that their nuclear physicists wouldn't be working with Iran. We forced them into the—into this relationship with Iran.

And I will tell you one other incident for the record, because I have been following this stuff, the Russians offered to back out of the agreement with the Iranians. I had this directly from players in this game, not Russians, but Americans. They offered to withdraw their agreement with the Iranian nuclear agreement if we would work with them on developing the next generation of nuclear power, which is safe and you can't melt it down, et cetera. And you know what? We turned them down. And we said, go play with the Iranians.

So a lot of the problems we have now, I think, have been based on we have not reached out to try to work with an honest discussion of differences with the country in which—yes, I am not trying to say that Putin is a democratic leader. He is oppressive and he has lied, and he is tied in the oligarchs that are crooked and draining the money from the Russian people, which should be used for their benefit. So I am sorry. I know it sounds like they are saying he is Putin's man. I am not Putin's man. But I am the only one who is willing to make the arguments on the other side and trying to see that in order to create a more peaceful world.

And so with that said, I am sorry I took up my whole 5 minutes.

Ms. ROS-LEHTINEN [presiding]. Thank you.

Mr. ROHRABACHER. I would let them refute me, and I will shut up.

Ms. ROS-LEHTINEN. Well, thank you. And we will let them do that, but let me go to Mr. Cicilline first.

Mr. Cicilline.

Mr. CICILLINE. Thank you, Madame Chair.

Thank you to our witnesses. I think one of the things that we understand is that our military is most effective when it works in conjunction with our diplomatic work and, of course, with our development professionals.

And I am just wondering whether or not any of the panelists think that it is possible for us to push back against Russian aggression and build the kind of competence in American leadership that we need through our military expenditures alone or should we, as members of this committee, continue to fight for robust investments in both foreign assistance and development aid that are such important parts of our foreign policy. As you might know, the President's budget proposes very deep, deep cuts in those areas. Yes? Everyone agrees?

Mr. KARA-MURZA. Thank you very much. And I want to just briefly say thank you for your kind words also during the introductory remarks.

I would like, Madame Chairwoman, if you would allow me very briefly to respond to what Congressman Rohrabacher said.

Ms. ROS-LEHTINEN. Yes. And I won't take from Mr. Cicilline's time.

Mr. KARA-MURZA. Thank you. First of all, it is very refreshing to see disagreement and genuine debate in a legislative body.

Mr. ROHRABACHER. Right.

Mr. KARA-MURZA. That is something we have long forgotten in my country. As you know, as a former speaker of the Russian Parliament, Mr. Gryzlov has said, Parliament is not a place for discussion. And, unfortunately, that is what it has become under Vladimir Putin.

The last time my country had anything resembling a free and fair election was more than 17 years ago, in March 2000. And this is not me saying it. This is according to observers from the Organization for Security and Co-operation in Europe. So when I say again and again that please don't equate Russia with the Putin regime, it means very simply that the current regime is not a product of Democratic election. It is not a product of a free choice of our people.

And you said, Congressman, one thing which I completely agree with. You said, let's not treat Russia with a double standard, and I think this is very important.

Mr. ROHRABACHER. Yes.

Mr. KARA-MURZA. We are not worse than you are. We are entitled to the same rights and freedoms that you have. Russia doesn't exist in a vacuum. Russia is a member of the Council of Europe. Russia is a member of the Organization for Security and Co-operation in Europe. We have clear international commitments with regard to such areas as free elections, freedom of assembly, freedom of the press, the rule of law and due process. The Putin regime has been violating these commitments and these principles for years, and it is not okay, if I could say this, for Western politicians, for Western political leaders to say, ah, forget it. You know, let them do whatever they want to do inside their country. Let's do realpolitik. Let's do business as usual with Mr. Putin. Let's deal with him as if he is, you know, a normal democratic-elected leader. That is not right. That is insulting. Because, you know, we have political prisoners in our country who are sitting in jails for their political beliefs.

Three days ago, we had peaceful opposition rallies on the streets of Russia, and more than 1,500 people were arrested and put to jail, including women, including teenagers. This is not okay. We have no freedom of the press in our country on a large scale. All the major media, all the major television networks are controlled by the government. And as I already mentioned, we have no free elections and have not had free elections for many years.

So I think it is very important to remember the values. You mentioned President Reagan several times today. And what President Reagan is remembered for in our part of the world is that he always attached great importance to values. And, yes, he engaged with the Soviet leadership on several areas, including arms control, but he also, every time he had a meeting with Soviet leader, he put on a list on a desk, the list of Soviet political prisoners, and he demanded their release. It would be nice to see something similar in terms of principles from the current generation of Western leaders. Thank you.

Mr. CICILLINE. Thank you. This is sort of building off of those comments. According to CNN, our President has spoken positively of President Putin over 70 times, calling him "highly respected within his own country and beyond" and saying he is doing, and I quote, "a great job."

I am wondering if you could share what you think the impact of that kind of posture by the American President is with respect to our allies in the region and with respect to our enemies in the region. What message does that communicate? It is sort of mystifying to me, but I am just wondering what are the geopolitical implications.

Mr. KARA-MURZA. Thank you very much. And, well, I think there is enough talk in this town about Russians meddling in your domestic policy, so I don't want to be one more. So I don't think it is my place to comment on, you know, the administration or any political dynamic in the U.S. But I would say this: I think, you know, if you watch Russian state TV, if you watch Kremlin propaganda outlets, you will hear that we, members of the Russian opposition, go to the West and we ask for money, we ask for political support, we ask for regime change. Of course, none of that is true. All we ask for are two things from Western leaders, including the Government of the United States of America, the most important democracy in the world. We ask only two things.

One is honesty, to be open and honest about what is happening in Russia. Don't pretend that something is happening that is not happening. Don't call things for what they are not. Just call things for what they are. Just be honest and open about the situation. That is the first thing.

And the second thing we ask for of Western leaders, including the United States, is please be true and be faithful to your own principles. Don't enable the export of corruption and abuse from the Putin regime to the West. Don't enable this behavior by providing havens, as so many Western countries have for so long, to those human rights abusers and those crooks and those corrupt officials from the Putin regime who steal in Russia but prefer to spend in the West and who keep their money in Western banks, who send their kids to study in Western schools, who buy real estate and properties and mansions and yachts in Western countries.

And the Magnitsky Act, which was passed by this Congress almost 5 years ago, which introduced this very concept of those people who engage in human rights abuse and corruption should not be allowed to enter the U.S. or use the U.S. financial system. Boris Nemtsov, who was already mentioned in these hearings, he and I were sitting in the House Visitor Gallery on the day the Magnitsky law was being passed. And I think every one of you present here voted for this law. And he called it, Boris Nemtsov called it the most pro-Russian law ever passed in a foreign Parliament, because it targets those people who abuse the rights of Russian citizens and who steal the money of Russian taxpayers. And that is commitment to principle. So this is all we would ask for of the U.S. Government or any other government in the Western world.

Mr. CICILLINE. Thank you. I have two other questions, and I am going to just pose them and you will have as much time as you need to answer them, I hope, Madame Chairman.

The first is how is Russia managing to pay for all of its costly interventions around the world, particularly in Syria, and to really begin to become even more engaged in the areas around the Middle East? Are they perceiving that they are getting a good return on their investment? And have the Russian people made the connection between a decline in their quality of life and Russian efforts in the Middle East? And does that either encourage the Russians to more deeply engage or what is the kind of long-term implications of that? Because my sense is they don't have the resources to do this without misleading the Russian people about the benefits of that.

And then the second thing is, we now know that Russian propaganda RT, a very powerful outlet for Russian propaganda, has an Arabic channel. And I would like to know a little bit about what Russia is investing in this propaganda in the Arab world and is it having an impact and what should we be doing and thinking about in terms of responding to the powerful spread of propaganda by the Russians through RT in the Arab world? So those are the two.

Ms. BORSHCHEVSKAYA. I want to respond to Congressman Rohrabacher. I agree with everything Vladimir said. I also just want to add very briefly in terms of President Reagan, you mentioned him a lot. President Reagan didn't only talk to the Soviet Union, he defeated the Soviets in Afghanistan. For example, he understood that military strength was also important. You know, and I as a child growing up in the Soviet Union, I——

Mr. ROHRABACHER. You know that I fought in Afghanistan against Soviet troops. You know that, okay?

Ms. BORSHCHEVSKAYA. Sure, but I just wanted to make that point.

Mr. ROHRABACHER. I was a special assistant to President Reagan.

Ms. BORSHCHEVSKAYA. Sure. No, I just want to highlight that point.

Mr. ROHRABACHER. All right.

Ms. BORSHCHEVSKAYA. And in terms of your earlier questions about engagement in the Middle East, the military and so forth, so first, one thing we can do is we can increase cooperation with our regional allies. And this doesn't require a lot of spending. We need to increase, for example, and I mentioned this in my testimony, increase port visits to the Eastern Mediterranean to enforce the notion with our regions that America supports our allies but it is not retreating.

The military could augment exercises beyond those that we already conduct with Morocco, Egypt, and Jordan and so forth. This is a small but very important, effective measure that we can take. More broadly, in terms of strategic thinking in the region, what the air strikes of April 7 have shown to Putin for the first time is that the United States will stand by certain red lines, that it is not just talk.

Unfortunately, it seemed that it was just a one-off, and as Brian had mentioned, we don't really seem to have a clear strategy. But if Putin understands that there is a clear strategy and that we will back up our talk with actions, that it is not just talk, that is incredibly important to curbing his influence in the region.

In terms of spending, in terms of how is Russia managing to do this, I don't have reliable numbers. I am not sure if anybody really does, because this is a very opaque system. Officially, what Putin had said is that Russia spent something around $400 million in March 2016. I suspect the real numbers are probably higher. That said, it is still not a lot, if you compare it to the Russian military budget. What he has been trying to do is do this on the cheap.

In Syria, for example, he let Iran do most of the heavy lifting, and this is why his interventions have worked so far for him. How long this is—whether or not it is sustainable, that is a different question.

And lastly, in terms of your question about RT Arabic, yes, RT Arabic is active in the region. It fuels conspiracy theories, frankly, just as it does in other languages. What we should do is not be on the defensive. We are always on the defensive. We are always trying to refute stories that RT puts out, and one reason for that, and I cited a report in my testimony, first impressions tend to be very resilient. And because Russian propaganda, Kremlin propaganda is not concerned with the truth, they often have a monopoly on first impression because they don't need to think about—investigate what really happened.

We need to work with our regional partners, perhaps establish outlets so that we cannot just be on the defensive but actually be on the offensive on this issue. Thank you.

Mr. CICILLINE. Thank you.

Mr. KATULIS. If I could add, your first question about the cuts and the proposed cuts on the State Department, in my opening statement, I characterized it as unilateral disarmament. And in the type of strategy that Russia has for engaging in the region it truly is unilateral disarmament. Just the assistance component of it. And, Congressman, you mentioned Christians in the Middle East, and it is something that touches my heart and we have done a lot of work on at the Center for American Progress.

Today, the fight in Mosul and Iraq, there is a postconflict stabilization effort where we are not even in the ball game that affects those communities. Some of the oldest Christian communities in the world over the last decade and a half have been run out of the region. And we know what it is like in human history to see when people are killed and murdered simply for what they believe in. And by unilaterally disarming, we are actually leaving those most persecuted and vulnerable populations, even more vulnerable, because others will fill the gap. In Iraq, it seems that Iran is coming in and trying to buy up property and things like this. And I think it is important for us to talk more about it.

Secondly, on the question of RT, I mean, it is of my view, and I mentioned for the last decade and a half, I don't think we have had a coherent strategy across the region, and that is especially the case in the battle of ideas, that after the 9/11 attack in our country here we had a lot of talk about how do you win that battle of ideas. And the latest episode we see I think coming from the Trump administration is his visit to Saudi Arabia and this new countering violent extremism center in Riyadh, Saudi Arabia, the image of the glowing orb, if you remember this.

This is a place where the United States and Congress needs to ask, what is going on there? What is our involvement? Where is the imprint of our values to talk about values? Where is the imprint of respect for religious minorities like Christians? Is that part of your conception of countering violent extremism in building this partnership with these countries? And I am all for building partnerships, I have written about it, with countries like this, but on our terms, not their terms.

Mr. CICILLINE. Thank you. And I thank the chair, and I yield.

Ms. ROS-LEHTINEN. Thank you, Mr. Cicilline.

Mr. Donovan is recognized.

Mr. DONOVAN. Thank you, Madame Chair. And I am so proud of the leader of our committee, our chairwoman, for being able to pronounce your names. It has taken me 2 years to say Ros-Lehtinen, and then she announced she is retiring after I got it down.

So I would just ask all of our panelists the same question. A lot of the conversation today has been about the administration's policies toward the Middle East, toward Russia. Besides restoring the proposed cuts in the budget, what do each of you think Congress alone could do to have an impact on many of the issues that each of you have brought to our attention today?

Mr. KARA-MURZA. Thank you. Congressman, thank you for the question. I think my answer would be to stay true to their values and just to remember the importance of the values, because actually a lot of—we haven't really touched on this today, but a lot of the actions that Vladimir Putin takes on the international arena and foreign policy is a direct continuation of what he does domestically in our own country.

I mean, if you look at modern Russian history, it has certainly been a pattern, a longstanding pattern that domestic repression eventually will translate into external aggression. Because after all, why should you expect a regime that violates the rights of its own people and that disregards its own laws to then respect other country's interests or international law? There is no reason. And, you know, those people in the leaderships of Western democracies for so many years, I must say, turned a blind eye to the abuses of democracy, human rights, and rule of law by Putin domestically. You know, the violations of freedom of the press, political prisoners, the rigging of elections and so on and so forth one day woke up to the external aggression of his regime in Georgia and the Ukraine, the annexation of Crimea, and now what he has been doing in the Middle East. These things are connected.

So I think it is very important to remember the importance of the principles and the values and issues such as rule of law, human rights, and democracy, both in your approach to U.S.-Russian relations and also to wider approach to foreign policy. And that is what I would say. Thank you very much for the question.

Mr. KATULIS. I have two very specific ideas. One, I think it is very important for Congress to consider a new authorization of the use of military force because of this creeping military escalation, that the U.S. actually has more forces nearer to the front lines of very complicated battles, and the legal frameworks that we are operating underneath are about a decade and a half old. And it is not just a legal issue; it is what is our responsibility as a nation to, when we are sending people into harm's way, to actually have a coherent understanding of the strategy from the administration. And I think having that debate over a new authorization can press this administration to clarify what it is doing.

Secondly, there are a number of arms sales that are proposed with partners in the region, and I have written before in reports like this that we need to use sort of these tools as leverage. We have an enormous amount of leverage. And in this year alone, I have been to Saudi Arabia, Lebanon, the UAE, Egypt, Morocco, a number of countries for my studies, and I have talked to most of the top leaders. And we are the strategic partner of choice, no matter what Russia has done in the last couple of years. We don't use those tools, including arms sales and military cooperation, to benefit stability.

So it is those two things. How do we use the tools in addition to the toolkit on the diplomacy and development? How do we use sort of the authorization for the use of force to press the Trump administration on what its Middle East strategy is? Because we could find ourselves in a shooting war with Iran directly at a moment's notice this summer or our troops at the receiving end of a chemical attack from ISIS. It is not inconceivable, but we aren't having that debate.

And then secondly, the levels of weapons sales that have been proposed, how does this fit within a strategic concept that brings stability to the region?

Ms. BORSHCHEVSKAYA. Yes. So I would just add so I think first authorization of use of force is very important. You know, one of the things that I highlighted in my testimony, and I just want to come back to that issue, Putin is trying—he is trying to limit our ability to maneuver physically, militarily in the region in the Middle East. He hasn't quite created full A2/AD bubbles. We can still operate, but now we have to think twice. He wants us to think twice. He doesn't want us to just—before, we were able to just go in and now we can't do that anymore. We have to think how is Putin going to react. For example, we use cruise air strikes. The reason why we are using them is because, again, we are afraid for our pilots.

So authorization of military use of force. And, you know, I agree with everything that Brian said. And I certainly agree very much with the issue of emphasis on values. Holding hearings like this, frankly, I think the hearing on Russia and the Middle East like this is way overdue. Putin has been involved in this region for a long, long time.

Lastly, I think sanctions, and we have seen this happen just this week. Congress is passing sanctions on Iran and Russia. So more conversations along those lines are very important. This is very concretely what Congress can do.

Mr. DONOVAN. Thank you to all of you.

Thank you, Madame Chair.

Ms. ROS-LEHTINEN. Thank you very much, Mr. Donovan.

And I will ask questions if that is okay, Mr. Cicilline?

Mr. CICILLINE. Of course.

Ms. ROS-LEHTINEN. Thank you. I have been in and out. I am sorry. Mr. Donovan did a very good job of holding down the fort.

Vladimir, you know the Putin regime and you have been a target of his repression. You understand the motivating factors for his actions. Can you tell us a little bit more about how Putin's domestic issues impact his foreign policy agenda? How important is it for him to be able to say that he beat the United States in Syria, for example? And what is his mindset when it comes to deciding when and how to intervene in many matters in the Middle East?

Mr. KARA-MURZA. Thank you, Madame Chairman, for this question. And as you know, the Putin regime has been described on many occasions as a virtual reality regime because it is so dependent on the propaganda image, on the television that—you know, the image that it creates itself. As you recall, one of the first actions of Mr. Putin in office was to shut down or take over all independent national television networks so that he would control the entire information picture, almost all of it.

And so I think it is sometimes underestimated in Western countries how much of what Putin is doing is actually geared for that domestic propaganda image. We already discussed this hearing, the relationship between his aggression against Ukraine and the domestic needs. He was very unhappy about this precedent of mass protests toppling a corrupt authoritarian government. And he was certainly not very happy or not at all happy about the prospect of something like this happening in Russia. And, again, he has been open about it. As we mentioned earlier during the hearing, he has himself compared the mass protests against his own rule in Russia to the one down in Ukraine to those color revolutions in post-Soviet countries, to the Arab Spring, and so on. So a lot of the aggression against Ukraine that he has been engaged in was motivated by domestic considerations to prevent the success of the democratic European experiment in Ukraine before it would become a model and inspiration for the same thing in Russia.

And as regards to Middle East and his involvement in Syria, if you watch Russian state television, which I would advise you not to do if you value your nervous system, but we have to, unfortunately, and if you watch it, you will see that most of it, most of the political talk shows, most of the news programs are dominated by the foreign policy agenda, by Putin's foreign policy adventurism. Before it was Ukraine, Ukraine, Ukraine and now in the last couple years it is all mostly Syria, Syria, Syria.

You are not going hear about economic problems in Russia. You are not going to hear about the sanctions that Putin himself introduced on the Russian people when he banned imports, for example, or food products from the U.S. and European Union 3 years ago. You are not going to hear about the problems with healthcare or education or the many social political and economic problems we have at home. All you are going to hear about, you know, are these reports of new military strikes, new bases, or new deals to make, you know, to extend the lease of Tartus and Khmeimim. You are going to hear about—you are going to see those images of Russian troops, Russian air space forces halfway around the world, you know, carrying out the valiant mission that President Putin has ordered them to.

You see this used for propaganda purposes 100 percent, and it is a very important reason in many ways for what Putin is doing to divert attention of the Russian public from the many problems at home and to back up the fraudulent, in my view, image that he has created of, you know, a Russia rising from its knees and being a great power again.

All I say to this is, you know, in the 1990s, which according to Putin were a time of humiliation for Russia when we had a democratic system of government under President Yeltsin, Russia was invited to join the G8, the most prestigious world club, the group of leading world powers. Under Vladimir Putin we were expelled from the G8, so where is humiliation in there?

Ms. ROS-LEHTINEN. Thank you.

Ms. Borshchevskaya, in case you want to chime in on that. Borshchevskaya. There we go.

Ms. BORSHCHEVSKAYA. No. I just want to echo what Vladimir said, and I always make the point, and this is why I said earlier in my remarks the blurred line between domestic and foreign policy in Russia. These are distractions and, you know, it is unclear how long Putin is going to be able to sustain this, but the fact of the matter is, up to date, he has been able to do that. And I think we need to recognize that, you know, we are in this for the long haul, that this isn't just going to disappear in a year or 2, that Putin is here to stay, at least in the near future, and we need to have a strategic, coherent response.

Ms. ROS-LEHTINEN. Thank you.

And finally, Mr. Katulis, you state that the leading powers in the region are engaged in a complicated struggle for influence, for power, and the key actors use a wide range of tools to assert their interests. Obviously, this is playing out between Saudi Arabia, UAE, Egypt, and Bahrain against Qatar, and there are concerns that this will align Qatar more closely with Iran. Russia and Iran obviously have a close relationship.

So do you think that there is a space that Russia will move in to take advantage of, and if, so how? How will it align itself with this power struggle? How should the U.S. move to prevent a potential Iran-Qatar-Russia nexus?

Mr. KATULIS. I think the first thing the United States should do is speak with a much clearer and coherent voice than it has. And I have met with officials from the Gulf in the past week from a number of these countries, and I think it is hard for most Americans to understand the complexities of the tensions there. It kind of feels like the Hatfields and the McCoys in Arabia because there is a history there and it goes back, and it is a little tribal. Yes, it touches upon perceptions of security threats and terrorism and things like this.

But bottom line, the number one thing I think the United States should do is have the senior figures in its administration, the Secretary of State, the Secretary of Defense, and especially the President of the United States, speak with a much more unified voice about this, and I think it is in their own self-interest. We have an administration which, again, I try to be clinical in my analysis and assessments, and I think it is still largely too early to tell what the complexion of the Trump administration's posture in the region will be. I think they have not sorted out a lot of their own internal sort of debates. Unfortunately, we have seen some of these internal debates sort of fully exposed on Twitter or in different statements or in different gestures.

So the most important thing to prevent a cohesive alignment there—and I don't think it is inevitable in any means, especially going back to a point I was making about weapon sales. The United States is about to sell billions more to Qatar, which is where we have a major air base. This is a point of leverage with all of these partners. We are better when our partners are unified, and a lot of the messaging and the gestures coming from the Trump administration just in the last few weeks cuts against the grain of what I think they were trying to do in talking about an Arab NATO and other things.

So a steadier approach, one where we are working together and trying to tease out all of these complexities, rather than create this unity or present this unity I think would be the most important thing.

Ms. Ros-Lehtinen. Well, thank you so much.

Thank you to all three of you. What excellent testimony, and we appreciate it. We hope to have a follow-up hearing on this. And thank you to the audience as well and the members of the press for being here.

And with that, the subcommittee is adjourned.

[Whereupon, at 3:38 p.m., the subcommittee was adjourned.]

APPENDIX

MATERIAL SUBMITTED FOR THE RECORD

SUBCOMMITTEE HEARING NOTICE
COMMITTEE ON FOREIGN AFFAIRS
U.S. HOUSE OF REPRESENTATIVES
WASHINGTON, DC 20515-6128

Subcommittee on the Middle East and North Africa
Ileana Ros-Lehtinen (R-FL), Chairman

June 8, 2017

TO: MEMBERS OF THE COMMITTEE ON FOREIGN AFFAIRS

You are respectfully requested to attend an OPEN hearing of the Committee on Foreign Affairs, to be held by the Subcommittee on the Middle East and North Africa in Room 2172 of the Rayburn House Office Building (and available live on the Committee website at http://www.ForeignAffairs.house.gov):

DATE: Thursday, June 15, 2017

TIME: 2:00 p.m.

SUBJECT: Russia's Strategic Objectives in the Middle East and North Africa

WITNESSES: Mr. Vladimir Kara-Murza
                     Vice Chairman
                     Open Russia

                     Ms. Anna Borshchevskaya
                     Ira Weiner Fellow
                     The Washington Institute for Near East Policy

                     Mr. Brian Katulis
                     Senior Fellow
                     Center for American Progress

By Direction of the Chairman

The Committee on Foreign Affairs seeks to make its facilities accessible to persons with disabilities. If you are in need of special accommodations, please call 202/225-5021 at least four business days in advance of the event, whenever practicable. Questions with regard to special accommodations in general (including availability of Committee materials in alternative formats and assistive listening devices) may be directed to the Committee.

COMMITTEE ON FOREIGN AFFAIRS

MINUTES OF SUBCOMMITTEE ON _____________ *Middle East and North Africa* _____________ HEARING

Day _____ *Thursday* _____ Date _____ *06.15.17* _____ Room _____ *2172* _____

Starting Time _____ *2:10 p.m.* _____ Ending Time _____ *3:37 p.m.* _____

Recesses |____| (____ to ____) (____ to ____) (____ to ____) (____ to ____) (____ to ____) (____ to ____)

Presiding Member(s)

Chairman Ros-Lehtinen, Rep. Daniel Donovan

Check all of the following that apply:

Open Session ☑
Executive (closed) Session ☐
Televised ☑

Electronically Recorded (taped) ☑
Stenographic Record ☑

TITLE OF HEARING:

Russia's Strategic Objectives in the Middle East and North Africa

SUBCOMMITTEE MEMBERS PRESENT:

GOP: Chairman Ros-Lehtinen, Reps. Steve Chabot, Adam Kinzinger, Lee Zeldin, Daniel Donovan, Ann Wagner, Brian Mast, Brian Fitzpatrick
DEM: Ranking Member Ted Deutch, Reps. Gerald Connolly, David Cicilline, Brad Schneider, Thomas Suozzi

NON-SUBCOMMITTEE MEMBERS PRESENT: *(Mark with an * if they are not members of full committee.)*

HEARING WITNESSES: Same as meeting notice attached? Yes ☑ No ☐
(If "no", please list below and include title, agency, department, or organization.)

STATEMENTS FOR THE RECORD: *(List any statements submitted for the record.)*

TIME SCHEDULED TO RECONVENE _____________
or
TIME ADJOURNED _____ *3:37 p.m.* _____

____
Subcommittee Staff Associate